Saint Joan of Arc

JOHN BEEVERS

Given to Alexandra on her Confirmation day by her parents.

property of: Mrs. Alexandra Tupy

TAN BOOKS AND PUBLISHERS, INC.
Rockford, Illinois 61105

Nihil Obstat: Gall Higgins, O.F.M. Cap.
Censor Librorum
Imprimatur: ✠ *Francis Cardinal Spellman*
Archbishop of New York
July 27, 1959

The nihil obstat and imprimatur are official declarations that a book or pamphlet is free of doctrinal or moral error. No implication is contained therein that those who have granted the nihil obstat and imprimatur agree with the contents, opinions, or statements expressed.

ISBN: 0089555-043-1

Printed and bound in the United States of America

TAN BOOKS AND PUBLISHERS, INC.
P.O. Box 424
Rockford, Illinois 61105
1981

CONTENTS

This is the story of a young girl who died when she was nineteen. She was no beauty and no scholar. She could neither read nor write. She came from the obscurity of a small, remote hamlet and in less than fifteen months had crowned a king, set in motion events that were to save her country from foreign domination, defeated the forces of a great nation, and changed the history of western Europe. She was burned to death as a heretic. Nearly five hundred years later she was canonized and became the patron saint of the country she saved. It is one of the most astonishing stories in history. This is an attempt to tell it simply but accurately and to peel away the smothering husk in which some historians have enclosed it. It is a task I have enjoyed and I hope that what I have done will enable others to feel the magic of those far-off summer days when this young girl, astride her charger, rode conquering through the fields and woods of France. But it is far more than the story of a conquest, far more than a medieval pageant. It is the story of a great saint—Joan of Arc.

1. The Girl

IT RAINED throughout the night. In the English camp the soldiers lay exhausted in their sodden tents. Some were ill; all were hungry, dirty, and unkempt. They had stormed Harfleur, losing many of their numbers in the business and many more had died of dysentery. They had set out to march to Calais to wait there until more men from England could join them. But the French set out after them and now they had caught them and there were three Frenchmen to every Englishman. There was jubilation in the French camp. At last, after many, many years of savage fighting, the English were to be destroyed.

The dawn came slowly, for the clouds were low and heavy with rain. The English rose and constructed before their ranks a palisade of sharply pointed stakes sloping toward the enemy. The archers assembled. Their weapons were a bow of yew wood five feet long and a bundle of arrows each two feet six inches in length, tipped with steel and flighted with the feathers of the gray goose. The arrows could drive through an armored breastplate and through the body of the man behind it. The English bowman was the most formidable killer in Europe. He did not look it. He was short and stocky, usually dirty and ill-shaven, wearing a patched or torn leather doublet and a rusty light helmet. He could, of course, neither read nor write. He drank a lot and swore more or less continually. His favorite oath was "God damn," which was so commonly on his lips that throughout France the English were called "Godons," the nearest the French could get to the native pronunciation. But he had no rival in the art of shooting an arrow with immense power, accuracy, and speed. The high, unending whistle of the English arrows was a sound of terror. For a century it had meant defeat and death. And, most important of all, the English bowman was the freest man—of his condition—in all Europe. He was not a serf. Nor did his king and the great barons despise him. They knew his worth too well. They were all bound together in a rough camaraderie. So on that gray autumn morning, king, lords, and bowmen faced the French, ready to die together but quite sure that, once again, victory would be theirs.

A spectator would not have had that certainty. The French were a formidable host, seemingly invincible. In immaculate armor, the chivalrous Frenchmen sat astride their heavy chargers. Very few men were on foot, only a handful of pikemen and the cross-bowmen who used the slow and cumbersome machine which fired a bolt released by a trigger. Banners and pennants were flying; there were shouts and laughter and the neighing of horses. All were well armed and supremely confident, and they outnumbered the English by three to one. All they had to do was to charge and trample the English into the mud. But, as even the most patriotic French historian admits, the leaders of the French at that time were stupid and incapable of learning the simple, bloody lessons the English had given them over and over again. They persisted in believing that battles were won by nobles encased in armor and sitting on steeds as strong as cart horses and not much more agile. They despised foot soldiers and made little use of them. If they got in their way during a battle, they rode them down.

And so, at about ten o'clock on that particular morning, they and their horses advanced to slaughter the English. A great line of metal-clad figures moved at a clumsy gallop across the soggy ground. It was magnificent, both as a spectacle and a target.

The English waited. At last, as the French lumbered within range, there came the growling shout, "For God, for Harry, and St. George!" and, as it died away, the thin whistle of the arrows. It was a very quiet business compared with a modern battlefield, quiet but deadly, and the knights of France began to tumble from their saddles. Those behind pressed on, riding over and crushing the fallen until they, in their turn, toppled down with an arrow through the throat or ribs. Straight and pitiless, the flight of the arrows never ceased, nor did the French advance. Those few riders who reached the English had their horses impaled on the sharpened stakes, and a dismounted man in armor was easy meat. When the English bowman had killed a fair number of the French and reduced the rest to a confused, leaderless mass, they dropped their bows, picked up billhooks, short-handled maces and knives, and sallied forth from behind their stakes. It was all over before the sun went down. Ten thousand Frenchmen were dead, many of them—against all the laws of war—having had their throats slit because they were not worth holding to ransom. Another thousand of the French were prisoners. The English lost just over a hundred men.

That day was St. Crispin's Day, October 25, in the year 1415, and the place was Agincourt.

It was a great victory, one of the many inflicted on the French since the battle of Crécy in 1346, when the English archers first showed their quality. It seemed that there was nothing to stop the whole realm of France from falling into English hands. But over on the other side of France a girl had been born less than three years before. Her name was Joan, and later she was to say to the English invaders: "Go away. For God's sake, get back

to your own country." It was not long before they went, driven
out by the victorious French. That the French were victorious
was due to one person and one person only—this girl.

Before we begin her story, there is some history to be mas-
tered. It is confused, full of squalid motives and not very in-
teresting, but without a knowledge of it we cannot appreciate
the greatness of Joan. No doubt we all knew something of this
history in our schooldays and no doubt we have all forgotten it.

On Christmas Day, 1066, William, Duke of Normandy,
was crowned King of England in Westminster, and for the
next four centuries France and England were closely linked, so
closely that at one time it seemed they might form one great
kingdom. In 1152, William's great-grandson, Henry II, married
Eleanor of Aquitaine and acquired her lands, so that he ruled
an area of France stretching from the English Channel to the
Pyrenees and from the Bay of Biscay to within—at one point—
a few miles of the Rhone. More than half France was ruled
by the King of England and, for many years, it was a situation
accepted without question by the French. But it was not des-
tined to last. French nationalism began to develop. There were
incidents, bitter quarrels and skirmishes—still very far short of
a major war, but serious enough for the two countries to sign
the Treaty of Paris in 1259, by which Henry II's grandson,
Henry III, handed vast areas of France back to the French
Crown and agreed that he would hold what he kept in homage
to the King of France.

All seemed settled. Edward I succeeded his father, Henry III,
and married the sister of the French King. He also married his
son to Isabelle, the daughter of the King. This son came to the
throne in 1307 and reigned as Edward II. From his marriage
with Isabelle of France he had, in 1312, a son who became King

of England in 1327. The next year the French King, Charles IV, the third king France had had in fourteen years, died, leaving no son. Edward at once claimed the throne of France through his mother, Isabelle, the sister of Charles. The French would have none of this and invoked the Salic Law, by which no woman could succeed to the throne of France. Edward argued that this law did not prevent his mother from transmitting the right of succession to him. But the French took Philip of Valois, the nephew of an earlier king, as their monarch, and Edward did homage to him, since Guyenne, the French province, still belonged to England. Then, however, Philip foolishly helped the Scots in another of the brawls that broke out between them and the English.

Even more important, France began to interfere in the affairs of Flanders. Wool was England's most important product. Nearly all of it was sold to Flanders and woven into cloth there. This trade was the keystone of England's economics. If Flanders were ever controlled by a hostile France, this trade would end and England's greatest industry would die. The Flemings themselves eagerly urged Edward to press his claim to the French throne. So, in spite of having paid homage to Philip, Edward decided to renew his claim and fight to establish it.

Thus began the Hundred Years' War. It opened in 1338 and ended in 1453. It was a most foolish and unnecessary war. France was reduced to extreme misery, and England was left with Calais as her only possession in France. But it was not a struggle that ended inconclusively. It established France and freed England from too intense a preoccupation with the mainland of Europe. Both these things could have been accomplished without such slaughter, and England must take most of the blame for this century of bloodshed.

Fortunately we need not begin to follow the fortunes of this war until it enters its closing phase. There were many skirmishes, many sieges, and many battles. There were truces and treaties, an occasional year or two of uneasy peace, acts of treachery and heroism—in fact, all the chaos and confusion, the material and spiritual jumble of any war.

Matters began to move slowly to their climax after Agincourt, and in 1420 there was signed the Treaty of Troyes. There were three parties to it: England, France, and the Duchy of Burgundy. (Burgundy, though legally a fief of France, was in fact an independent and powerful state and an ally of England.) By this treaty, Henry V of England assumed the title of Regent of France and heir to its throne. He was to marry Catherine, the daughter of the King of France, Charles VI, and succeed to the throne on the death of Charles. The treaty went on to exclude from the succession the son of Charles VI, the seventeen-year-old Charles, the Dauphin. Henry married Catherine. He had a son by her and then, in 1422, he died. Two months later Charles VI of France died. So the political situation was suddenly and disastrously altered, as the new King of England, Henry VI, was a baby of nine months. By the Treaty of Troyes, he was also King of France.

The Dauphin, now nineteen, was the true King of France by right of inheritance, but the Treaty of Troyes had dispossessed him. Yet half France accepted him as King; the other half, led by Philip, Duke of Burgundy, was determined that he should never reign. The Duke of Bedford, uncle of the infant Henry VI, governed as Regent that part of France held by the English. The Dauphin kept himself south of the river Loire. It is highly probable that if Henry V had lived until his son reached manhood, the whole of France would have accepted this son as the legitimate King, for he was, after all, half a Valois. That, however, is one of the innumerable "ifs" of history. As it was, France was as divided territorially, politically, and emotionally as she was during the Vichy regime of the last war.

In the northeast of the country was the hamlet of Domrémy. Half of it was in France, half in the Duchy of Bar, a duchy supporting the Anglo-Burgundian cause. The hamlet stood on the left bank of the river Meuse. The crest of the slope rising from the opposite bank marked the boundary of the Duchy of Lorraine. In Domrémy lived a small farmer named Jacques or Jacquot d'Arc, a native of Champagne. He was married to Isabelle Romée, who came from a village a mile or two north of Domrémy. Their neighbors considered them "good and pious Catholics and good farmers, of good reputation and an honest way of life, but not very well off." The couple, it is true, were far from rich, but by the standards of the neighborhood they were not poverty-stricken. They had a house, a garden, some livestock, and were rudely fed and roughly clothed. As far as their physical conditions of life were concerned, we should consider they lived a brutish and squalid existence. Their house was small, dark, and damp with an earthen floor; chickens wandered in and out and rushlights or a smoky fire gave the only light at night. Close by the door was a great dungheap. The food was coarse, with meat only on the great feast days. They washed rarely and were lousy. But we need not pity them for all this. No one has ever been made any happier by bathtubs and fluorescent lighting.

On January 6, 1412, a daughter was born to them. They already had two boys and a girl, and a third boy was to be born later. This second daughter, born on the feast of the Epiphany, was baptized in the church of St. Rémy near her father's house. She was named Jeanette. After she had left Domrémy for good, she was always called Jeanne. The English-speaking world calls her Joan. She grew up without ever going to school and could neither read nor write. Later she learned to trace her name and signed the letters she dictated. Her mother taught her the Our Father, the Credo, and the Ave Maria and she heard many stories about the saints. When she grew older she began to work, helping with the spinning and cooking and going with her father and brothers to the fields and weeding and digging there. She also took turns at tending the cattle the villagers turned loose to graze in the river meadows. One of her friends said of her: "She was brought up as a good Christian and was a model of good behavior. She gave alms for any money her father could spare her. She liked going to church and went a good deal. She went gladly to confession, and I often used to see her kneeling before the priest. We were always telling her that she was too pious. She was a hard worker and did every kind of job about the house, and she was always spinning." Another friend declared: "Joan was good and sweet. She was often embarrassed by what people used to say about the number of times she went to church." It must not be thought from this testimony that she was a little prig. Devout and good she certainly was. She was also very gay and lively. She ran races with the other village girls and took part in all the village festivals.

Near the village was a great beech tree known as *L'Arbre des Dames*, or "the Ladies' Tree." Report had it that in the olden days fairies used to visit it and spend the night dancing around its massive trunk. In the neighborhood there were also wells and streams said to be the haunts of the fairies. On Rogation Sunday, the whole village, led by the priest, used to go in procession to these streams and wells and to the Ladies' Tree, and the priest read extracts from St. John's Gospel at each halting place, as this Gospel was considered particularly efficacious in banishing every kind of spirit. On Laetare Sunday, the fourth Sunday in Lent, the young people used to visit the tree and dance under it and picnic there. They gathered wild flowers, made garlands of them, and hung them on the tree. They paid similar visits on the great feast days later in the year. Joan went with them and "behaved just like the others," according to one of her godfathers. But her visits to the tree were not so frequent as those she made to a little chapel in the woods about a couple of miles from her home. It was dedicated to Our Lady of Bermont and had a statue of Our Lady and the Child Jesus which was credited with miraculous powers. She went there regularly, either alone or with Catherine, her elder sister.

But her days were not an uninterrupted business of work, prayer, and games. Domrémy and the surrounding district were not exempt from the horrors which were sweeping France. Everyone lived in a state of alarm, and day and night one of the villagers kept watch from the church tower, ready to ring the bells the moment he caught sight of any troops. Joan's father, acting for all the villagers, had rented an abandoned castle on an island in the Meuse, and on more than one occasion all the villagers and their cattle fled to this stronghold and stayed there until a band of marauding soldiers had passed through Domrémy, looting it as they went. Once a knight and his followers descended on the village before the alarm could be given. They stripped the houses of their wretched furniture and drove off all the cattle. Joan was thirteen when that happened. The husband of one of her godmothers was carried off in another affray and had to be ransomed. The husband of a cousin was killed. They were not regular armies which caused such distress, but bands of armed ruffians who gave only a nominal allegiance to the two great warring parties. They spent their time looking for ill-defended villages to plunder, and what they could not carry off they usually burned. In 1428, the church at Domrémy was burned to the ground and the crops in the fields destroyed. So Joan grew up in the midst of violence. She never, because of her station, knew a comfortable life; because of her country's plight, she never knew a peaceful one.

In the summer of 1424—the actual month and day are unknown—all was changed for Joan. And the history of Europe was changed.

Joan was twelve when she experienced the key event of her life. She herself has told what happened: "I was in my thirteenth year when a voice from God came to help and guide me. At first I was very frightened. This voice came about noon in summer when I was in my father's garden. I had not fasted the day before. I heard the voice coming from my right from the direction of the church. I rarely hear it without seeing a light, and the light—always very bright—comes from the same side as the voice."

This statement is an irritating one. It leaves so much unsaid and we, more than five hundred years later, want to know every detail of this first hearing of her guiding voice. But, although she disappoints us here, she makes amends later when she is on trial for her life. Then, in answer to the questions of the prosecution, she gives, as fully as she can, an account of these visitations. Here is a summary of her account, assembled from her replies.

At first the voices urged her to be good and go to church. It was at this first hearing that she vowed to remain a virgin as long as it should please God. The third time she heard the voice she knew it was that of the archangel Michael and she saw him accompanied by many angels. She saw them with her bodily eyes. When they left, she wept and wished they had taken her with them. Later St. Catherine and St. Margaret habitually appeared. They addressed her as Joan the Maid, daughter of God—*Jeanne la Pucelle, fille de Dieu.* They wore beautiful crowns. St. Michael forewarned her that they would appear to her, and told her she must follow their counsel and that she must believe all they said, as they were speaking for God. She did not know if their hair was long, nor whether they had arms or legs or, indeed, any human, physical features. When asked the foolish question: "How could they speak if they had no mouths?" she said, "I leave that to God." She was also asked if St. Michael was naked. She replied, "Do you think God has not the means to clothe him?" She touched St. Catherine and St. Margaret. They had a fragrant smell. The voices came to her usually when the church bells were rung. The sexton sometimes forgot to ring them punctually and she gave him little cakes she had baked herself to bribe him into strict regularity. As time went on, the voices ceased to give her general exhortations to lead a virtuous life and issued orders for precise action: "Daughter of God, you must leave this village and depart into France. You must lead the Dauphin to Rheims, where he may be rightfully crowned." She was also told that she would raise the siege of Orléans and that, through her, Charles would rule over the whole of France. If we believe her, at the time she was told about Orléans the town was not under attack, nor did it seem likely that it would be. But she did not disclose anything about Orléans until it was besieged, so we should not make too much of this apparent foreknowledge.

Here we have got to decide whether or not we believe in these voices. The Church lays no compulsion on us in this matter. Joan of Arc was canonized for the heroic sanctity of her life. Her voices were not mentioned during the examination of the career that led to her being raised to the altars. So we are free to accept the voices as Joan accepted them—real voices, the voices of an archangel and two saints, with their words inspired by God—or treat them as auditory hallucinations. Yet, even though we are free to choose, or rather, because we are free, we cannot, I think, maintain an attitude of detached neutrality. Our intelligence will nag away at us until we make up our minds either for or against.

Let us first of all see why Joan should say she saw those particular three—St. Michael, St. Catherine, and St. Margaret. We must try to understand the medieval mind. To that mind, angels were not theological abstractions. An angel was—as indeed he is—a created being of supernatural power, charged by God with duties toward the members of the human race. That we should believe and no doubt do, but I should be surprised if, to many of us, angels play as real a part in life as they did to the men and women of the Middle Ages. To them, angels were almost tangible presences. They were always at hand, ready and eager to help all who called on them, and they had the power to do so. And the archangel Michael was the greatest of them all, the prince of the heavenly hosts. Holy Scripture calls him the "guardian angel of the people of God," and the Fathers are unanimous in hailing him as the protector of the Church, which has two feast days in his honor. In the fifteenth century, all Christians knew this, but those Frenchmen who were loyal to Charles had a particular devotion to St. Michael. In the Middle Ages, all countries put themselves under the protection of a saint. The English had St. George, whom they invoked as they went into battle. They called on him with a great shout and believed that it was he, under God, who gave them the victory.

In their early history, the French had dedicated their kingdom to St. Martin, and his shrine in Tours was the greatest center of pilgrimage in the country. Later St. Denis, an early bishop of Paris, who was said to have been martyred there, became the patron saint of France. But the House of Valois adopted St. Michael. His great shrine was in Brittany—Mont-Saint-Michel. Vast bodies of pilgrims started making their way there in the fourteenth century, and in the 1390's boys between the ages of eleven and fifteen assembled in all the towns of France and made their way to Brittany in spite of the general insecurity and consequent hazards of the journey. Charles VI increased this devotion. For much of his life he was mad, but in 1394 he made a pilgrimage to Mont-Saint-Michel and for some time afterward was sane. In gratitude he renamed one of the gates of Paris. Porte d'Enfer—the Gate of Hell—became Porte Saint-Michel, St. Michael's Gate.

A few days before Charles VI died, the Dauphin was in La Rochelle and banqueted there with many nobles. The banquet hall was on the first floor of the château and, halfway through the meal, the floor collapsed. Many were killed and many injured. The Dauphin escaped without a scratch. He declared he owed his safety to St. Michael. This incident took place on October 11, 1422, and a few months later he ordered that every year on that day there should be a Mass celebrated in every church in honor of St. Michael for his intervention and to beseech him to save the kingdom and deliver it from its enemies. This, of course, was known in Domrémy.

In August, 1424, the Duke of Bedford launched an attack on Mont-Saint-Michel from the land, but the English were beaten back. It was about this time, during her third hearing of the voices, that Joan saw St. Michael. Next year, the Duke of Bedford, still maintaining his ring of blockading forces around the land side of the Mont, assembled a great fleet to blockade it from the sea. The place was completely surrounded and its ultimate fate seemed inevitable. But the defenders of the Mont appealed for help to the seamen of St. Malo. The appeal was answered with speed and resolution and in June, 1425, a fleet under the command of the Admiral of Brittany attacked the English ships riding at anchor off Mont-Saint-Michel and destroyed or captured them all, with the exception of three or four that managed to put out to sea and escape to England.

It was the first important victory over the English gained by the French for half a century. Only six years earlier, in 1419, Henry V had captured the great abbey of St. Denis and seized the oriflamme, the standard of France. It seemed to everyone that France had been abandoned by St. Denis. If he would not preserve his own sanctuary, was it to be expected that he would save France? St. Michael, though, seemed as if he were prepared to use his flaming sword for the Valois and for France. And it was in this year, when the abbey of St. Denis fell to the English, that the Dauphin's standards were adorned with the figure of St. Michael killing with his sword the serpent under his foot.

Joan was not plagued by newspapers, telephones, news broadcasts, and the television screen, but news traveled very quickly. Domrémy, though only a hamlet, stood near an important road along which passed a steady stream of pilgrims, friars, merchants, and, of course, refugees seeking safety. The news of great events was never very long behind their happening. It is very certain that everyone in France was fully aware that the kingdom had been placed under St. Michael's protection and that he had already shown his power. So it is not surprising that Joan identified the chief of her visitants as the archangel; nor, on the other hand, is it strange that it should be in fact St. Michael who came to her.

As for the other two saints, in the Middle Ages they both enjoyed an extraordinary devotion—extraordinary, considering how little was known about them. How little, that is, of historical fact. Here, though, we must remember that the people of that period accepted legend as fact, and the more fantastic the legend the more eagerly was it accepted. So Joan would know all about St. Catherine. Born in Alexandria about the year 313, St. Catherine was the daughter of a king of Egypt. She was baptized by a hermit and had a vision in which Jesus married her and placed a ring on her finger. The Emperor Maximinus ordered that a great sacrifice should be made to the heathen gods and that all the Christians of Alexandria should take part in the ceremony.

Catherine went to the temple where the animals were being sacrificed, demanded to see the Emperor, and then attempted to convince him of the truth of Christianity. He produced fifty of the philosophers and rhetoricians attached to his court and ordered them to convert her to paganism. Her arguments converted them to Christianity. The Emperor put forward another fifty. They, too, became Christians. Maximinus thereupon had the whole hundred burned alive. Catherine was flogged and flung into prison. There she was visited by the Empress, and Catherine's eloquence converted her. When Maximinus heard of this, he executed his wife and offered to marry Catherine if she would forsake her faith. She, of course, refused and was bound between wheels armed with spikes designed to tear her to pieces. But a thunderbolt fell on the device and destroyed it, leaving her unharmed. She was at once beheaded, and angels carried her body to Mount Sinai. It is a picturesque story but is unsupported by a single fact.

St. Margaret was the daughter of a heathen priest of Antioch, but her nurse was a Christian. When her father discovered this, he turned both of them out of the house, and Margaret was reduced to tending sheep with her nurse. The Prefect of Asia, one Olybrius, passed by and saw this girl of great beauty amidst her sheep. He asked her to marry him. She refused and told him she was a Christian. He put her to the torture and then flung her into prison. There the devil appeared in the form of a dragon and swallowed her. She crossed herself and the dragon burst, leaving her unhurt. After fresh tortures she was bound and flung into a great vessel of water. She prayed that this might be her baptism, and immediately there was a great earthquake, the vessel was shattered, and a dove carrying a golden crown alighted on her head. Finally she was beheaded. In the fifth century, Pope Gelasius—not surprisingly—rejected the whole of this story, but the Crusaders of the eleventh century came back to the West full of the legend, and a great cult to her developed.

It is certain that Joan would know every detail of the legendary lives of these two saints. She could not read, but she would hear stories about them from the village priest and all the wandering friars who passed through the neighborhood. To-

day many a teen-age girl thinks and dreams of film and television stars; Joan's imaginings were concerned with saints who,
although their lives were legendary, taught the lesson of
constancy unto death and of unshakable devotion to God.

Now, were these three figures—St. Michael, St. Catherine,
and St. Margaret—hallucinations, or did they really appear as
objective figures? Were their voices noises in a disordered
head, or were they supernatural utterances? Or was Joan lying
and did she really hear nothing?

The one thing that is quite certain is that she was not lying.
Young women do not die at the stake rather than confess to
such a lie. The voices could, though, have been hallucinations.
It is obvious that Joan was not a normal girl. To say this is not
to imply in any way that she was mad or even slightly unbal-
anced. No saint is normal or, to use the word properly, perhaps
it is only the saints who are normal. Generally we use the word
wrongly, saying it when we should say average or ordinary.
It is certain that Joan was an extraordinary person, and equally
certain that some extraordinary persons have hallucinations.
It is, however, a fact that if anyone has hallucinations, those
hallucinations will not remain quiescent. They will not, that
is, be like dreams. They will. act upon and influence the
sufferer's whole character.

A soldier is given an order by his superior officer. He obeys it,
but it does not change his whole nature. His way of thought
and feeling remain the same. So it was with Joan. Her voices
told her to do certain things. She obeyed, but she did not suffer
that change of character which is so noticeable when we
examine the behavior of those who merely imagine they hear
voices.

There is always a disintegration of character in the victim

of hallucinations. It is not always immediately obvious. The afflicted person may seem to have a strong will and great determination of purpose, but this particular inflexibility is a pitiable and evil thing. It yields to neither reason nor emotion. It is mad. The victim of hallucinations also may become confused, weak, and irresolute, swept this way and that by his disordered mind. Whatever the change caused by hallucinations, it is always one for the worse.

Joan's voices impelled her to action and guided her whole life, but they did not, as it were, spill over and stain her character. She had great strength of will, but she remained humane. She was determined but never arrogant. She never behaved like a fanatic. She wept when she was hurt, liked to ride a fine horse, joked and laughed and rejected all the adulation offered her. She had no formal learning, but her wits were exceedingly sharp. From time to time she lost her temper, but never her humility. Even if we did not know that she was a saint, we could not fail to see her as a good and able young woman with a character remarkable for its steadiness and balance. There is not the slightest trace in her of those defects that hallucinations always cause.

Are we to accept that her voices came from God? I see no reason for hesitation. I am not concerned with attempting to convince those who, if they saw the heavens rolled away, would think it a trick of the light or an advertising stunt. I am presuming that we accept that God sometimes communicates directly with human beings, to deny which would be to deny God and His omnipotence. In the case of Joan, there have been objections to the use of the archangel and the two saints for the strange reason that these three figures must, before the coming of the voices, have held a dominant place in her imagination. It is thought that the fact that she knew so much about them must inevitably make suspect her story that they came to her as supernatural messengers. Actually, it is just the reverse. God could have spoken to her without any intermediary, or He could have used any intermediary He chose—from one of her father's sheep to any of the birds fluttering in the hedges. But the story of God's dealing with those he selects for a special task is not a fairy story, nor is it something out of the *Arabian Nights*, where fishes speak and dogs sing. God never acts in a bizarre manner. Throughout all history, the miracles He performs have about them a sanity, a balance, a rightness, which stamp them as His work. St. Michael, St. Catherine, and St. Margaret were familiar friends of Joan's. Their message astonished her. Her humility would not at first allow her to imagine that she could obey that message, but she was not astonished or frightened by their appearing to her. As always, God used the most suitable form of approach.

When we consider that Joan died rather than deny the reality of her voices; that, under their influence, she changed the future of the Western world; that at all times she showed great common sense, was lively and spirited, humble and good, we can, I think, be sure that she was not a deluded girl; that she was what she said she was—the agent of God.

How did she react to the voices? Her initial fright soon vanished, but her bewilderment at the orders given her remained for many months. When she was told: "Daughter of God, you must leave your village and go to France," she protested, "But I'm only a young girl, and I cannot ride or fight." Nor could she understand how she was to lead the

Dauphin to Rheims and have him crowned there. For more than three years she stayed in Domrémy and heard the voices several times a week, a gentle, persistent, heavenly nagging. Her piety increased, but she seemed to get no nearer fulfilling the mission given her. At last, however, she was told the step she must take: "Daughter of God, go to Robert de Baudricourt in the town of Vaucouleurs that he may give you men to take you to the Dauphin."

Vaucouleurs was a small town on the Meuse, a few miles north of Domrémy. It was loyal to the Dauphin and commanded by this Robert de Baudricourt, a seasoned warrior who, by a combination of fighting and intrigue, had succeeded in keeping his royalist outpost out of the hands of the enemies of France.

Joan, obedient to her voices, determined to visit him and ask for his help. Before we accompany her on her journey, let us pause for a moment to try to get a picture of this young girl. What did she look like?

There is no authentic portrait of her, although the whole of France is dotted with lumpy statues of an armored woman on a horse which are intended to represent her. All we know of Joan is that her hair was black and cut short. Her complexion was dark and presumably sunburned and generally weatherbeaten. She was rather short. There was nothing masculine about her voice; it was soft and womanly. She was strong, able to ride hard and long and wear armor for nearly a week at a stretch. No one ever said she was beautiful. She appears to have been a stocky peasant girl, used to hard work and the open air.

2. She Sets Out

JOAN KNEW that her father would refuse to allow her to go to Vaucouleurs, but her mother's cousin, Jeanne, lived in the hamlet of Burey, midway between Domrémy and Vaucouleurs, and was married to Durand Laxart, a man sixteen years older than Joan. So Joan asked if she could pay a short visit to these relatives. It was only a short visit—a week during the middle of May, 1428. Toward its end, Joan suggested to Laxart that he should escort her to Vaucouleurs and into the presence of Robert de Baudricourt.

When she told him why this journey was essential, Laxart must have been extremely disturbed by this proposal. He was a farm laborer; Robert de Baudricourt was an aristocrat with the power of life and death over him. For Laxart to appear with his young cousin and tell de Baudricourt that she could save France and needed his help was a very formidable undertaking, for Robert de Baudricourt was a choleric soldier and not to be trifled with. Yet Laxart was more easily persuaded to help Joan than a farm laborer of today would be. The people of the fifteenth century had a fervent, unquestioning belief in God and knew that He often intervened in their affairs through a chosen agent.

Today Joan would have been thought mad. Would anyone have helped such a girl to approach the Prime Minister of Britain or the President of the United States during the last war on the grounds that she could end the struggle and bring them victory? It cannot be imagined. Five centuries ago, however, it would have entered no one's head to deny that God could choose a girl and give her power to save her country. There was only one thing the men of that age wanted to be absolutely certain of: if a girl claimed to enjoy supernatural guidance, were her claims genuine? Was she guided by God or the devil?

So Laxart's prime concern was only whether this particular girl, Joan, would be believed. Nowhere in France or in the whole Western world would he have been met by complete, instant, and automatic certainty that she was a lunatic and that, in the very nature of things, all she said was untrue and her claims impossible. The principle of divine guidance was accepted everywhere; only its particular manifestation might be challenged. Still, it needed courage to escort her to Vaucouleurs, for Robert de Baudricourt would give short shrift to an impostor and to whoever introduced her.

Laxart had that courage. One morning—the exact day is not known—he and Joan (she was wearing a worn red dress) climbed the hill above Vaucouleurs on which Robert de Baudricourt's fortress stood. Once again we notice the difference between that age and this. The fortress gates were open and people were going freely in and out. There were no security passes to be shown, no forms to be filled in, no uniformed guards to escort every visitor. Laxart and Joan walked through the courtyard and into the great hall where Robert was sitting and talking with his men-at-arms.

She went straight up to him and with no formal greeting said at once, "My Lord has sent me to you to tell you to send word to the Dauphin that he should remain ready but not engage his enemies. My Lord will help him before Lent ends." She went on, "The kingdom does not belong to the Dauphin, but my Lord wishes the Dauphin to become King and to hold the realm in trust. The Dauphin will be made King in spite of his enemies and I myself will lead him to be anointed and crowned."

Robert asked her, "Who is this lord you speak of and what right has he to give orders to the King?"

Joan's answer was, "The King of Heaven."

In these four words we hear for the first time the authentic voice of Joan—assured, blunt, simple, and direct. Never does it vary. It always has the ring of authority. But on this first visit of Joan's to Vaucouleurs it had no effect. Robert de Baudricourt told Laxart to take her away and back to her father who, if he had any sense, would give her a good thrashing to drive her foolish fancies out of her head.

So Joan went home. We know nothing of her reception there. Very soon after her return, the English and the Burgundians decided to reduce the handful of loyalist strongholds in the Meuse valley and, by June 20, Vaucouleurs was invested. The inhabitants of Domrémy realized that their village could not remain unscathed, so they assembled their cattle and their goods and went off to the town of Neufchâteau, some seven or eight miles to the south. Joan and her parents stayed at an inn for a week or two. During her stay Joan confessed more than once to Franciscan friars. When she was on trial for her life, her accusers alleged that this inn was no better than a brothel and that Joan spent a lot of time with the girls living there. This, like most of their allegations, was a lie.

When the people of Domrémy returned home, they found their village a heap of burned-out ruins. Even the church had been destroyed. Vaucouleurs was unharmed. It had been conditionally surrendered under a sensible medieval custom which saved much life and suffering. The leader of the garrison of a besieged town parleyed with the besiegers and told them that he had enough supplies to hold out until a certain date. If he were not relieved by that date, he would surrender the town. If they accepted this offer, the besiegers would leave the town in peace, generally sending off their main forces to seek fresh conquests. They returned on the appointed date. Such agreements were never broken. There is no record of the date on which Robert de Baudricourt offered to surrender Vaucouleurs, but he was still in possession of the town in the middle of Lent the following year.

Meanwhile more English troops had landed in France and, joining their fellow troops already there, they began to march toward the Loire. In October they began their siege of Orléans. If it fell, the whole of France was open to them. Joan felt she must act at once, but she had to wait until January. She knew that Laxart's wife was due to have a baby in that month, and it had been arranged with her parents that she would go and make herself useful about the house at that time. In the middle of January, Laxart arrived to escort her. Still wearing her worn red skirt and in a shepherd's cloak, she left Domrémy. She never saw it again. She was just seventeen.

Before she left to meet the Dauphin, she spent six weeks in and around Vaucouleurs—a few days with Laxart and his wife, some weeks in the house of Catherine Roger and her husband, who were friends of the Laxarts, and a day or two was spent on a visit to Nancy.

Once again she visited Robert de Baudricourt. This time much of his skepticism had gone. It is easy to see why. He had made a conditional surrender of his town, the English were advancing everywhere, and the loyalist cause seemed almost lost. He was, it is obvious, ready to clutch at a straw. The powers of earth were failing him, perhaps those of heaven might help, and perhaps this peasant girl was their agent. But he had to make certain of that, so he took a priest with him and went to see her in her room at the Rogers'. The priest put on his stole and ordered her to depart if she were possessed by an evil spirit but to approach them if her inspiration came from God. She fell on her knees and shuffled across the room to them, displaying none of the signs which, in that age, were accepted as proof that one was possessed by a fiend—there were no contortions, foaming at the mouth, or obscene blasphemies. But Joan was angry with the priest, for she had been to confession to him and knew that he must know she was neither possessed nor planning any evil.

It was at this meeting with Robert de Baudricourt that Catherine Roger heard Joan say to him: "I must go to the Dauphin. Haven't you heard the prophecy that France would be ruined by a woman and saved by a virgin from Lorraine?" But Baudricourt still hesitated. He now had no thought of dismissing her as he did on her previous visit to him, but he would not yet provide her with an escort for her journey to the Dauphin. We cannot be sure why he hesitated and why he finally yielded, but it seems probable that he sent word about Joan either to the Dauphin or to one of his immediate circle and then sat back and waited for orders as to what to do with her. But this is mere guesswork. It is probable, but there is no evidence for it.

During this period of waiting—which, according to Catherine Roger, Joan found "as wearisome as does a pregnant woman"— two men lost all their doubts and pledged themselves to her. They were Jean de Metz, aged twenty-eight, and Bertrand de

Poulengy, aged thirty-six, both of good families and both attached to Robert de Baudricourt's garrison. Jean de Metz, moved solely by curiosity, went to see her at the Rogers' house. He has told what happened:

"I said to her, 'Well, *ma mie*, what are you doing here? Must the King be driven from his realm and must we all become English?' And the Maid answered me, 'I have come to speak to Robert de Baudricourt to ask him to take me or have me escorted to the King. But he pays no heed to me. Yet before mid-Lent I must be with the King even if I have to wear my legs down to the knees. For there is no one on earth, neither king nor duke, nor the King of Scotland's daughter [she was referring to the recent betrothal of the Dauphin's son, who became Louis XI, to Margaret, one of the three daughters of the King of Scotland], nor any other person who can restore the realm of France. Only I can do it, yet I would much sooner stay at home and help my mother with her spinning, for I am not cut out for this kind of life. But I must go and I must accept the burden, for it is the will of my Lord.' I asked her who her Lord was. She said, 'He is God.' And then I put my hand in hers to pledge my faith and swore that with the help of God I would lead her to the King. I asked her when she wanted to start. She said, 'Better today than tomorrow, and better tomorrow than later.' Then I asked her if she wanted to travel in her woman's clothes. She said she would rather be dressed as a man, so I gave her a suit and breeches belonging to my servants. After that some people of Vaucouleurs had a man's suit and breeches and everything else that was necessary made for her, and they gave her a horse which cost about sixteen francs."

We do not know what it was about Joan that impressed Bertrand de Poulengy, as we have no record of any talk he had with her, but he too pledged himself to get her to the King.

Before the time came for them to fulfill their pledge, there was a curious episode. Joan was summoned by the Duke of Lorraine to his court at Nancy. Jean de Metz accompanied her to Toul, halfway there, and Laxart made the whole journey with her. There has been much speculation as to why the Duke, a supporter of the Burgundians, should show such interest in Joan, particularly as she visited him under a safe-conduct and he made no attempt to detain her. It seems, however, that in this matter he was not concerned with politics. The state of his health worried him more than the condition of France. He was sixty-three and ill. He had taken as his mistress a young woman, Alison Dumay, the illegitimate daughter of a priest. He had had five children by her and was still infatuated by her. Ill and, by the standards of that age, a very old man, he was tormented by the thought that if he died unreconciled with his wife he would go to hell and equally tormented at the prospect of putting aside his mistress. He was determined to get well and so postpone the day when he would have to reform his life and repent his sins.

He had heard of Joan, and rumor had turned her into a wonder-worker. She was summoned to his court to heal him. When she arrived, she told him bluntly that he was a sinner and that he would not be cured until he amended his life. She had no powers of healing, but it was possible that God, in His mercy, would cure him if he dismissed Alison and restored his wife to her rightful position. She then asked him to let her have an escort to conduct her to the King and that the escort should be commanded by his son-in-law, René d'Anjou. In return, she would pray that he might be cured.

This request, astonishing in its audacity, is typical of Joan, who was always completely unmoved by rank and power except in so far as she could use them to serve God's purpose. The Duke of Lorraine was very far from being the kind of duke we know today; those amiable, powerless English dukes, for example, who earn an honest dollar or two showing visitors around their faded ancestral homes. Within his territory the Duke was all-powerful and reigned as an absolute monarch. Yet Joan told him he was a sinner and must repent, then went on to demand his support for an enterprise which, if it were successful, would threaten his reign and duchy. Charles, however, as if too astonished at her temerity to take offense at it, merely refused to help her, but he did give her four francs and a black horse.

On her arrival back in Vaucouleurs, Joan saw Robert de Baudricourt again and said, "I call God to witness that you have delayed too long. The Dauphin has this very day suffered a great reverse near Orléans and he will suffer many more unless you send me to him." The day was February 12, 1429. Several days later news of the Battle of the Herrings reached Vaucouleurs. The French had attacked an English convoy bringing supplies to the forces besieging Orléans. (Barrels of salted herrings were among the supplies, hence the name of the battle.) Once again the English archers had slaughtered the French. Here was a clear case of second sight. We do not know whether it was this or whether a message from the French court had at last reached Robert de Baudricourt, but, whatever the reason, he at last decided to send her to the King.

Joan swiftly made her preparations. She had her thick black hair cut in the fashion of a soldier, a style that in the fifteenth century was as hideous as the crew cut of these times. She wore a shirt, breeches, doublet, black hose fastened to the doublet with twenty laces, and long leather boots with spurs, and carried a short black riding cloak. On her head she had a black woolen cap.

Her companions and escort were Jean de Metz, Bertrand de Poulengy, their two servants, an archer named Richard and Colet de Vienne. This last was a royal courier, and his presence indicates that messages about Joan had been exchanged between Vaucouleurs and the court.

Some of her friends tried to warn her of the dangers ahead and painted a grim picture of a devasted countryside thick with rapacious and lecherous soldiers. She was unmoved and declared, "I care nothing for soldiers. The road lies before me, and if I encounter armed enemies God will strike a way for me through the midst of them, for I must go to the Dauphin, since it is for that that I was born."

At last the day of departure came; Wednesday, February 23. It was a gray morning, cold and misty, and just after dawn the little cavalcade assembled at the Porte de France. Robert de Baudricourt fastened a short sword in Joan's belt and made each man take an oath that he would protect her and get her safely to the Dauphin. The portcullis rattled up and the drawbridge was lowered. Robert de Baudricourt, who was never to see her again, raised his hand in farewell and cried, "Go! Go! And let come what will!"

The little group of riders, with the seventeen-year-old girl at its head, moved off and was soon lost in the mist.

The rescue of France had begun.

3. The King

By THE first night of their journey they had reached the Abbey of St. Urbain. They stayed there and in the morning heard Mass before crossing the Marne. The land across which they traveled was desolate. Cultivation had ceased except around fortified towns and castles, open land was overrun with briars, and woods were thick with undergrowth and tangled, untrimmed saplings. And each one of them knew that capture meant death. Joan's only concern, though, was that she could not hear Mass every day. "She often said to us," Jean de Metz records, "'It would be a grand thing if only we could hear a Mass'." Sometimes they traveled at night, sometimes by day, and slept in the open. Jean de Metz says: "On the way, Bertrand and I slept each night with her. She slept beside us without taking off her doublet and breeches. I was in such awe of her that I would not have dared to go near her and, on my oath, I never had any desire or carnal feelings for her." Bertrand de Poulengy also says: "Every night she slept with Jean de Metz and me, keeping on her surcoat and her breeches laced and tied. I was young then, but I had no desire or carnal urge to touch her as a woman. I would not have dared to approach her, because of the great goodness I saw in her. I never saw any badness in her. She was always such a virtuous girl that she seemed like a saint."

It was a rough journey. The weather was very cold and the ground frozen. They could never light a fire lest its smoke should betray them. Their food was probably hard bread, salt fish, and dried meat. The men, professional soldiers, were hardened to such a life, and for Joan, toughened by the every-day roughness of medieval times, it cannot have been the ordeal it would be for a modern girl. She never lost her cheerfulness. When her companions, particularly Jean de Metz, questioned her about her mission, "she always told us not to be afraid, since she was commanded to do this. For her brothers in Paradise told her what to do, and it was four or five years ago that these same brothers and God had first told her that she would have to go to the war to restore the kingdom of France. And I had a great trust in what she said and I was on fire with her words and with a love for her which was, I believe, a divine love. I believe that she was sent by God."

For eleven days they rode on. They heard Mass at Auxerre and reached the Loire at Gien. Once across the river, they were in the King's territory, though not out of danger. Some soldiers, nominally loyal to the King, set out to meet Joan with the intention of kidnaping her and holding her to ransom, but "at the moment when they were about to do so, they found themselves unable to move, so Joan escaped together with her company." Finally they arrived at Fierbois, the great center of devotion to St. Catherine. Joan dictated a letter to the King, announcing her arrival and asking permission to come to him at Chinon. Colet de Vienne rode off with it. Joan went to church and heard three Masses, one after the other. This church stood on the site of a chapel founded in 732 by Charles Martel, who presented his sword to it in thanksgiving for his great victory over the Saracens when they had thrust up through France as far as Poitiers and were threatening the whole of Christendom.

That same evening, Colet de Vienne returned from Chinon bringing permission for Joan and her party to enter the little town. They set off next morning and arrived about noon. She was lodged in an inn and waited there two days until the summons came from the King. It was in the late afternoon when she rode up the steep hill to the castle where Charles held his ineffectual court. As she was about to cross over the drawbridge, a mounted soldier stared at her and called out to his companions a coarse and degrading remark in her regard, punctuated by words of profanity. Joan reigned in her horse and turned in her saddle. She looked at him for a moment, then asked, "Why do you take God's name in vain when you've so little time to live?" She rode on into the courtyard. Within an hour the soldier had slipped and fallen into the river and was drowned. A rather savage punishment for a medieval wolf-whistle, though perhaps Joan's words were a prophecy and not a judgment.

Within the castle the King was awaiting her. He was twenty-six. His father was a madman, his mother a monster of lust and cruelty. In person, he was thin, with spindly, bandy legs, thick lips, watery eyes, and a long, bulbous nose. Both pious and superstitious, he heard three Masses a day and constantly consulted astrologers and soothsayers. He was cowardly and irresolute. Years later he became a good and able king, but at the time of his meeting with Joan he was a pitiable specimen.

Their meeting took place in the Hall of State, lit by fifty torches and crowded with some three hundred nobles. It is one of the great moments of European history: Outside was the darkness of a winter evening and the darkness of a ravaged country near complete overthrow and conquest, a darkness that was pressing in on the little court and threatening to overthrow it. Most of the men in the hall were well-muscled but brainless courtiers, brave and stupid hangers-on. A few were potential traitors, ready the moment they could be quite sure they were making no mistake, to desert the King and make the best terms they could with the enemy. A few more—a very few—were brave, intelligent, and loyal. Their devotion was to France and, hard though it was at times, they saw France in the weak and ugly mannikin they called the King. To them, out of the darkness, appeared this new, strange ally—a young, illiterate peasant girl, ignorant of war and politics; ignorant of everything, in fact, that men of affairs thought essential. Into the hall she came, short, stocky, clothed like a man, her face grave and brown, topped with her thick black hair cropped like a boy's.

There is a story that when she went up to the King and knelt before him he pointed to one of the nobles and told her that he was the King. She was not deceived and declared: "In God's name, you are the King and none other." This is one of the stories that gets into history books for tiny tots, but there is not a scrap of reliable evidence for its truth. Joan herself never mentions such an incident, nor do the only three men who were present and afterward gave evidence about the meeting.

In fact, she advanced straight to the King and said, "Gentle Dauphin, I am Joan the Maid. God has sent me to you to help you and your kingdom. You shall be anointed and crowned in the city of Rheims and you shall be the lieutenant of the King of Heaven who is the King of France."

Charles gazed at her uncertainly, then led her aside and talked privately with her. "And after hearing her, the King appeared to be joyous," the assembly remarked when he rejoined them. Charles had asked her to give him proof that she truly had a mission from God. She told him that on All Saints' Day of the preceding year he had gone alone into his oratory in the castle of Loches and had prayed for a long time; prayed silently, uttering no words. She told him this and what his prayer was. From that moment Charles had complete faith in her. He was to vacillate, to hang back and to display all his inherent weaknesses, but from that moment he never wavered in his belief that she was an agent of God.

The Middle Ages, however, were not peopled by credulous fools as we, through a wholly imaginary superiority, are inclined to imagine. Some of the people of that time had beliefs we may think foolish, though why we, who believe that all wisdom comes out of a ballot box, should smile at a medieval thinker declaring that kings are divinely appointed is beyond my comprehension. We cheerfully entrust the running of our daily lives and the future of our country to politicians who are usually distinguished neither by great virtue nor high intelligence, yet we wonder that Charles placed the fate of France in the hands of Joan. But Charles, though personally accepting her, behaved with vastly more caution than any modern electorate. After this first meeting he handed her over to an investigating committee and waited for their verdict before giving her a shred of power.

It is necessary to hammer away at this point about the Middle Ages in any book dealing with them which is written to be read in the United States and England. Much sentimental nonsense has been written about this period. Words could not express the horror I should feel if I were transported back to the Middle Ages and had to live out the rest of my life amidst their filth and squalor. Life then was mostly short, dirty, and painful. Certainly in England, the only country of which I can speak with authority, the poorest worker of today enjoys far greater comfort than any medieval prince could ever hope to know. But we must not fall into the common error of judging the past by the standards of the present. Happiness is not rendered impossible by the absence of television sets, deep-freezers, and automobiles. Great things have been done by men who ate with their fingers. So we must put aside our neurotic preoccupation with hygiene and our pride in technology when we look at the France of Joan of Arc. Because so many of the things and ideas which are commonplace to us were unknown to the people then does not mean that they were simpletons. Many of them had subtle and searching minds. They exercised them on theology and philosophy, not on science. They were more concerned with the Trinity than with neutrons. They concentrated on the means of attaining eternal bliss, not immediate destruction. Being human, they made mistakes and the means they chose were sometimes wrong, but their goal was the right one. And it was before a body of such educated men that Joan appeared.

She was escorted to Poitiers, for it was there that most of the exiled members of the University of Paris had gone, and Parliament had been moved there. She stayed with one of the King's lawyers, Jean Rabateau, and his wife. The council of investigation was headed by the Archbishop of Rheims, Regnault de Chartres, who was also the Chancellor of France. Among the members of the council were several professors of theology. The Dominicans, Carmelites, and Benedictines were represented, and there were authorities on civil as well as canon law. These men examined Joan for about three weeks. The record of this examination has been lost or destroyed, and all we know of what was said comes from the evidence given at the trial for Joan's rehabilitation by Seguin de Seguin, a Dominican friar and professor of theology. He was a leading member of the Poitiers council. A contemporary account calls him "a very sour man"—an unjust verdict when we consider his patience under Joan's reply to his questions. He asked her: "What kind of language do your voices speak?"

Her reply, "A better one than yours," must have brought a smile to many faces, for Brother Seguin admitted: "And indeed I speak with a Limousin accent." Undeterred, he asked her whether she believed in God. "Yes," she replied, "more than you do." He then told her: "God cannot wish us to trust you unless He sends us a sign to show that we should believe in you. We cannot advise the King to give you soldiers merely because you ask for them." Joan's patience grew a little thin: "In God's name, I have not come to Poitiers to produce signs. Lead me to Orléans and there I will show you the signs for which I am sent." Then, in the words of Brother Seguin, "she prophesied to me and those others present four things which happened as she foretold. First she said that the English would be beaten, that the siege of Orléans would be raised and the town rid of the English. Then she said that the King would be anointed at Rheims. Third, she said that Paris would return to the King's rule and, last, that the Duke of Orléans would come back from his captivity in England. And I have seen all this come true."

Another Dominican professor of theology then tackled her: "You say your voices tell you that God wishes to deliver the people of France from their distress. But if he wishes to deliver them, there is surely no need of soldiers." To which Joan replied, "The soldiers will fight and God will give them the victory."

When she was confronted with books of theology, she declared, "Our Lord has more books than you possess. He has a book no priest has ever seen."

That is all we know of this investigation at Poitiers, except, of course, that the men conducting it came over unanimously to the side of Joan. They said, "Now, seeing that the King has made trial of the Maid, as far as he is able, and that he finds no evil in her, and that she declares she will give a divine sign before Orléans, and seeing how persistent she is and how consistent are her words and that she is urgent in her request to be sent to Orléans so that she can show there that the aid she brings is from God, we believe that the King should not hinder her from going to Orléans with soldiers, but that he should send her there and trust in God. For to fear or reject her when there is no sign of evil in her would be to rebel against the Holy Ghost and to render oneself unworthy of divine aid." They declared that they had reached this conclusion after "examining her life, her conduct, and her intentions," and finding her "in all things humble, virgin, pious, honest, and simple."

Before they signed this report, they had Joan examined by several women, including the Queen of Sicily, the King's mother-in-law. These women declared she was "wholly and utterly virgin, without trace of violence or corruption." This verdict was of supreme importance, for it was a cardinal belief of the time that the devil could have no dealings with a virgin. By itself, Joan's virginity did not make her worthy of trust, but it did guarantee that she was not a witch.

During these weeks in Poitiers, Joan, quite certain that the reality of her mission would be recognized, dictated a letter to the English. It was headed "Jesus-Maria" and read:

"King of England and you, Duke of Bedford, who call yourself Regent of the realm of France, and you, William de la Pole, Earl of Suffolk, John Lord Talbot, and you, Thomas Lord Scales, who call yourselves lieutenants of the Duke of

Bedford, hand back to the Maid, who is sent by God, the King of Heaven, the keys of all the fine towns of France you have taken and ravaged. She is ready to make peace if you return to France all you have stolen from her. And you, archers and soldiers, noble or not, who are before the city of Orléans, go in God's name back to your own country. If you stay, await news of the Maid, who will very soon come upon you to your very great hurt. King of England, if you do not do what I ask, I will force your men to depart wherever I meet them in France; if they do not, I shall have them all slain. God, the King of Heaven, has sent me to drive them out of France, but I will show them mercy if they obey me. Do not believe that it is from God that you will hold the kingdom of France, for it is King Charles, the true heir, who will so hold it. That is the will of God, revealed to the King by the Maid. And the King will enter Paris with a goodly company. And if you refuse to believe these words from God and the Maid, we will fight you wherever we find you. If you will not do what is right, there will be a greater uproar than France has known for a thousand years. You can be very sure that God will give such powers to the Maid and her good soldiers that you will find them invincible, and battle will show to whom God gives the better right. And you, Duke of Bedford, the Maid begs and prays that you will not force her to destroy you. If you will do what is right, you may accompany her to where the French will do the noblest deed ever accomplished for Christianity. [Joan is here referring to a crusade against the Turks.] Tell me if you want peace in Orléans; if not, remember that great trouble will be upon you soon."

It is an astonishing letter for a seventeen-year-old girl to have sent to a great lord, the Regent of a king and commander of victorious armies. It was dictated by Joan in Poitiers but was not sent until a little later.

From her arrival in Chinon to the end of her examination at Poitiers, her time had not been wholly spent in being proved and tested. She made one good friend, the Duke of Alençon, a handsome young man in his early twenties. His father was killed at Agincourt and the English had killed his great-great-grandfather at Crécy. He arrived at Chinon the day after her first meeting with the King and they took an instant fancy to each other. He says: "I was out hunting quail when I heard that a maid had come to the King to tell him that God had sent her to drive away the English and raise the siege of Orléans. So I went to the King next day and found Joan talking to him. She asked who I was, and when the King told her she said to me, 'You have come at a good time. The more of the blood royal there are together, the better.' Next day the King, the Duke, Joan, and a few courtiers went into the meadows round the castle. Joan leaped on a horse, seized a lance, and gave so skilled an exhibition of tilting with it that the Duke there and then presented her with a magnificent horse."

It is a pleasant picture: a morning at the very beginning of spring, the young, richly dressed men, and Joan, lively, uninhibited, on a proud, curvetting charger, showing off, I'm afraid, to the laughter and applause of the spectators. Certainly that morning sealed her friendship with the Duke of Alençon. He never wavered in his devotion to her, and to Joan he was always *mon beau duc*—my good duke. A little later she went with him to stay for a day or two with his wife, who told Joan how afraid she was lest any further misfortune should befall her husband. He had, she pointed out, been captured at the battle of Verneuil in 1425, had spent five years as a prisoner of the English, and had been released only on payment of a crippling ransom. Joan told her, "Don't be afraid. I will return him to you safe and sound, just as he is now or in even better shape."

There was nothing sexual in the Duke's devotion to Joan beyond, of course, what is inevitable in the most platonic of relationships between a man and a woman. He himself says: "I never had any carnal desire for her."

After Poitiers, Joan was taken to Tours and provided with a little household of her own. She had two pages, Louis de Contes and Raymond; a squire, Jean d'Aulon, a man greatly trusted by the King; a confessor, Jean Pasquerel; an Augustinian friar; and, of course, Jean de Metz and Bertrand de Poulengy, the two young men who escorted her from Vaucouleurs to Chinon. In addition, she was joined by her two brothers, Pierre and Jean.

It was at Tours, a town famous for its armorers, that a suit of armor was made for Joan, a suit of plain, unadorned steel. A sword was offered her, but she refused it, saying she knew of a better one. She dictated a letter to the priests of the church of St. Catherine at Fierbois, the church where she had heard three Masses on her way to Chinon, telling them to dig behind the altar for a sword they would find there, on which five crosses would be engraved. A messenger carried this letter to Fierbois, and the priests dug and found the sword engraved with five crosses. It was thick with rust, but it was cleaned and found to be in perfect condition. The priests of Fierbois enclosed it in a scabbard of scarlet velvet. At Tours, another scabbard of gold cloth was provided, but Joan had a stout leather sheath made for it.

No rational explanation has ever been given of this episode. It is certain that no legend existed about the presence of such a sword. It has been suggested that Joan hid it herself during her visit to the church. Such a suggestion is absurd and shows the lengths to which skeptics are driven by their denial of the supernatural. For one thing, it would be at complete variance with everything we know of Joan's character; and for another, it is not conceivable that she could arrive at Fierbois with such a sword, bury it, and go on to Chinon without her companions being aware of its absence. It is equally inconceivable that, even if they knew she had buried it, they would not have disclosed their knowledge, perhaps not immediately, but certainly when they were giving evidence about her on oath during the investigation which was begun to rehabilitate her twenty years after her death.

In Tours, too, a standard and a pennon were made for her. The standard was a square of buckram fringed with silk. On one side God, pictured as the King of Heaven, was shown holding the world in one hand, with the other raised to give a blessing. On one side of Him knelt the archangel Michael, on the other Gabriel. They were offering Him a lily. The words "Jesus-Mary," in letters of gold, stretched above the whole design. On the other side of the standard was a silver dove bearing in its beak a streamer carrying the words "Through the King of Heaven." Her pennon, a small triangular flag, depicted Our Lady with an angel kneeling before her and presenting her with a lily. Both standard and pennon were painted by Hamish Power, a Scot who lived in Tours and painted signs for a living.

It was from this town that she dispatched to the English the letter she had dictated at Poitiers. Then she moved to Blois, where men and material were being assembled for the assault on the English investing Orléans. She stayed there two or three days and had another standard made. This bore the image of Our Lord crucified. Round it she assembled all the priests with the French forces each night and morning during her campaign, and they chanted anthems to Our Lady. Soldiers were welcome at these gatherings, provided they had confessed.

What, at this moment, was the situation at Orléans? The English had arrived before it in October of the preceding year. It lay on the north bank of the Loire, roughly rectangular in shape, some twelve hundred yards long and five hundred yards deep. Its walls were thirty feet high and four feet thick. Twenty-four towers rose from them and in the whole circumference there were five gates. In normal times the town had a population of some fifteen thousand. Now it was greatly swollen by an influx of refugees from the devastated countryside around it, and some estimates put the number of people crammed within its walls as nearing forty thousand.

As soon as the English forces settled down before it, they set about trying to cut it off from any possibility of receiving outside help. It must be admitted that the English were not very able at the business of besieging towns. They had been for a hundred years incomparable in a pitched battle, but they usually proved great bunglers when they squatted outside a well-fortified town. They were clumsy and dilatory, without enthusiasm and behaving as if they had all the time in the world.

At Orléans, they began building wooden forts in a ring around the town, erecting them on the main roads leading from it and putting one or two on the south bank of the river. These forts were badly sited, being so far apart that the occupants of one could not go quickly to the help of those in another. Nor was stabling provided, so the men inside a fort could only sally out on foot. Just over two miles to the east of Orléans, one of the forts was built on the north bank of the Loire, but between this fort and the one across the Paris road to the north of the town, there was a three-mile gap and no fort was ever built in that gap. It was, it is true, patrolled by the English, but in a most slipshod manner, so that provisions were always slipping into the town. In March, for example, six horses carrying herrings, six carrying gunpowder, and some cattle entered Orléans; in April the town welcomed fifteen oxen, one hundred and eighteen pigs, many bushels of wheat, much miscellaneous food, and several barrels of gunpowder.

The people of Orléans were always hungry, but starvation was a long way off. Their greatest discomfort was that caused by overcrowding. Had it been summer, disease would have killed them off like flies. They realized this, hence the urgency of the messages they sent the King asking him to send an army to relieve them. Nor did they enjoy having great stone cannon balls crashing among them from time to time, shattering the roof of a house or smashing a man to pieces. It was, though, a fairly courteously conducted siege. On Christmas Day, the English asked the French to lend them some musicians, and an orchestra was sent from the town to the enemy headquarters, where it played for several hours. On another occasion the commander of the town sent a fur wrap to the Earl of Suffolk in return for a basket of figs. But these little civilities did not lull the fears of the citizens of Orléans. They knew that the town must fall before the

English could overrun the whole of France, and so they knew that the English would ultimately reinforce their besieging army and finally batter their way through or over the walls. They knew, or perhaps sensed instinctively, that the battle for Orléans would be decisive and, with the succession of French defeats sharp in their memory, were defiant but pessimistic.

We must not be misled by the sizes of the forces engaged. Although forty thousand people may have been crammed inside the town, only about three thousand men were trained, professional soldiers. Another five thousand men—a kind of citizen-militia—were able to perform some defense tasks, though they would have been of little use in hard hand-to-hand fighting. Joan led another three thousand men into Orléans, so the French force consisted of some six thousand soldiers and five thousand other men who were useful but not frontline troops. The English had ten thousand good soldiers.

If we think only of numbers, the relief of Orléans was a very small affair when compared with the key battles of the ancient world or with such bloody fields as Waterloo. Let us keep in mind the words of the English military historian, Edward Creasy, who said in *The Fifteen Decisive Battles of the World:* "It is not because only a few hundred fell in the battle by which Joan of Arc raised the siege of Orléans that the effect of that crisis is to be judged . . . it may be asserted without exaggeration that the future career of every nation was involved in the result of the struggle." And a greater than Creasy, the Scotsman, David Hume, declared: "The eyes of all Europe were turned toward this scene where, it was reasonably supposed, the French were to make their last stand for maintaining the independence of their monarchy and the rights of their sovereign." I give these opinions because when we come to the fighting at Orléans there are moments when we seem to be reading of some confused and trivial brawl which no history book should trouble to record. Many a skirmish in the last war cost more in men and material.

Inside Orléans there was great joy and excitement when it was learned that Joan was on her way. One of its citizens, a cloth merchant named Jean Luillier, said: "Her entrance was greatly desired by everyone, because of her fame and the rumors about her. It was said that she had told the King she was sent by God to raise the siege, and the people were so hard pressed by the English that they did not know where to turn for help except to God."

4. The Victory

ON APRIL 27, 1429, the French army left Blois for Orléans. The priests were in front, bearing Joan's standard and chanting the *Veni Creator Spiritus*, with the soldiers following and six hundred provision and ammunition wagons and four hundred head of cattle bringing up the rear. In the company were some of the great warriors of the kingdom—the Admiral of France, the Marshal of France, the Lord de Rais, who, like Joan, died at the stake though condemned on a very different charge—that of conducting diabolic rites which involved the slaughter of many children. Today, he also lives on, but as the fairy-tale monster, Bluebeard. There was, too, Etienne de Vignolles, known as La Hire, a famous and able mercenary, renowned for his bravery and the vigor and fluency of his oaths. He and Joan became great friends, but he had to cease his cursing. All she would allow him to use was her own expression, "*En nom Dieu*"—in God's name. Perhaps a prayer he always said before going into battle appealed to Joan, for it has about it the kind of tough, robust piety we sense in her: "Lord, I pray You to do for La Hire what he would do for You if You were a captain and La Hire were God." He was no toady. He once asked the King to make an immediate decision about an important matter. Charles brushed this matter aside and asked La Hire for help in preparing a fête. La Hire exclaimed: "I think no one could lose a kingdom more lightheartedly than you."

The Loire is a lovely river. It winds its long way through the heart of France; broad and, except in a season of flood, clear and shallow, with low green islands lying on its easy-flowing surface. Round about Orléans, willows and poplars fringe its banks. To the utilitarian, industrial man it is quite useless: it turns no turbines and floats no tankers. And so its beauty now must be little changed from the days when Joan marched along its southern bank to the liberation of Orléans.

The relieving force slept in the fields the first night out from Blois. Joan remained in her armor and woke bruised and sore. By the second evening they had reached a point just beyond Orléans. When she discovered exactly where they were she was enraged by what she considered the perfidy of the army's leaders. Medieval armies made no use of maps, and Joan knew nothing of the topography of the neighborhood. She had left Blois believing that she was leading the army straight to the enemy. Now she saw a river between her and the main English forces. No one had, in fact, deceived her. The army and its leaders considered they were thrusting straight to the English, as indeed they were, but they would also have considered it an act of supreme folly to arrive before the strongest English positions encumbered with wagons and cattle and outnumbered by more than three to one. If the advance had been made along the north bank of the Loire, they would have faced the main body of the English firmly established in a strong arc between them and the walls of the town and would inevitably have been cut to pieces. It seemed far better to the French to travel along the river's south bank, but a little way inland from it; then, when just past the town, to descend to its banks and cross it and approach Orléans from the east, the side almost free of English surveillance. It was a decision which made sense five hundred years ago and still does today.

The commander of the Orléans garrison came across the

river to greet Joan. He was the Bastard of Orléans, the Count of Dunois. The illegitimate son of Louis of Orléans and cousin of the King, he was twenty-six and, with the Duke of Alençon and La Hire, was unshakably loyal to Joan. He tried in vain to rescue her after her capture. That, apart from an equally vain attempt by La Hire, was all that was ever done to snatch her from the stake. Their first meeting was not a happy one. Joan asked, with little graciousness in her voice, "Are you the Bastard of Orléans?"

"I am, and I rejoice at your arrival."

She asked him another question: "Is it your doing that I came here on this side of the river? Have you prevented me from marching straight to where the English are?"

Dunois declared, "I believe and so do other wiser and more experienced men that we have done the best and wisest thing."

Joan then burst out, "In God's name, Our Lord's advice is better and wiser than yours. You thought to deceive me, but you have only deceived yourself, for I am bringing you help more powerful than any soldier or city can give you. It is the help of the King of Heaven. It comes, not because of me, but because God Himself desires it. He has heard the prayers of St. Louis and of St. Charlemagne and has had mercy on Orléans. He will not allow the enemy to hold both the body of the lord of Orléans and his town." (The lord of Orléans was the Duke of Orléans, who had been a prisoner in England since his capture at Agincourt. Dunois was his brother.)

It was dark and heavy rain was falling. Dunois, of royal blood, commander of the beleaguered town and perhaps the ablest of the King's soldiers, had ignored his birth and military rank to make the hazardous journey across the river to greet this peasant girl. As he stood in the rain, his welcome was met by a torrent of abuse and he was called to account like the meanest of his soldiers. He knew also, of course, that Joan's desire to advance straight upon the English was, by all human standards of prudence, the sheerest folly and almost certain to lose Orléans. But there was something about the wet and tired girl that killed any anger he might have felt at her arrogance. It was not because she had been sent by the King, who so far inspired neither respect nor fear among his nobles. Joan had authority. Everyone who came in contact with her felt it. It was that completely assured authority which comes from the knowledge that one is an agent of God, acting in direct and immediate obedience to His commands. Joan always made it very plain that the King was her secondary master; she served him and his cause only because that was the task God had given her.

Meanwhile, on that wet and stormy night, there was work to be done. It had been arranged that boats should leave Orléans and go upstream to take on the provisions brought from Blois. But the wind was blowing strongly downstream and, as the river was low, they could not tack against the current. It looked as though the provisions would lie there until the English attacked and captured them. The military leaders conferred, but there was nothing they could do. Far across and down the river the barges were waiting, huddled against the town walls, useless hulks until the wind changed. Joan, who took no part in this conference—she was, perhaps, sulking a little—finally asked them what they were looking so disturbed about. Dunois told her. She laughed: "Is that all? The wind will change." And change it did, almost as she spoke.

A great deal of rubbish has been written about this. No one disputes that the wind did change, but those who seek to strike out the supernatural in Joan's life declare that there was nothing strange about this almost instantaneous veering of the wind. They say that Joan, a country girl, would know long before the marshals and commanders when a change in the weather was imminent. This is balderdash. Those who put the theory forward show that their ignorance of medieval life is matched by their ignorance of weather conditions. Dunois, La Hire, and the rest of them had lived as much in the open air as Joan, and for longer. Unless they were cloistered monks, medieval men spent most of their days out of doors in all seasons. Also, in western Europe there is no wind that blows steadily and strongly from the east and, in a second or two, swings around and blows just as strongly and steadily from the west. Dunois and his men knew this as well as any meteorologist. And they were astounded. Dunois was convinced there and then that Joan was no ordinary girl and that God was acting through her. He says: "I had great hopes of her from that moment." It was a conviction that never wavered. He at once crossed the river to where the barges were waiting and led them up and across to where the provisions had been stowed. They were quickly loaded and taken safely downstream to the town, moving at one point within cannon shot of one of the English forts.

This inertia of the English is hard to understand. No one who had campaigned against them ever accused the English commanders of giving their opponents the slightest chance when they came across them in the open field. Yet this small French force, cluttered up with wagons and stores, had traveled from Blois quite unmolested. Their advance was reported by English scouts and they would have had no chance against an English onslaught. Dunois himself, before he met Joan, had thought it needed only two hundred Englishmen to scatter a thousand Frenchmen. It passes all belief that the English watched the barges assemble, saw them held back by the wind, watched them set out, and saw them return loaded high with stores for the town—and did nothing. The English were victorious in a score of battles, they feared no French army, they greatly outnumbered the force from Blois, and they well knew the importance of Orléans. Yet they sat in their forts and in their camp, apparently disinterested observers of all the coming and going. They could have captured the stores and destroyed their escort with ease. Joan's confessor, Brother Pasquerel, says: "The astonishing thing is that the English, with their great forces well armed and ready at all times to join battle, saw our men—a very small company compared with them—and heard the chanting of the priests (I was in the middle of them, carrying the standard), and yet not an Englishman stirred and they made no attack on the soldiers and priests."

With the provisions safe, Dunois returned to Joan. He had the difficult task of explaining to her that the accompanying force was to return to Blois but that she must cross the river and stay in Orléans. It seems that not one of the French leaders ever saw this force as anything but an escort. Once it had fulfilled this function, it was to march back to Blois, cross the river there, and then advance on Orléans along the north bank of the Loire, the route Joan believed it was taking when it first set out. Joan objected strongly to this proposal. Dunois reports: "She made difficulties. She said she was reluctant to see her soldiers go, as they were all well confessed and repentant, and so she did not want to leave them and enter Orléans. I went to the captains in command of the soldiers and begged and commanded them, in the name of the King, to agree to Joan entering the town while they and their soldiers returned to

Blois." From this it appears that, just as Joan did not want to leave the soldiers, they were equally reluctant to part with her. But Dunois finally persuaded them and they came to Joan and told her: "Go in good heart, for we promise we shall soon be back with you."

So she reluctantly crossed the river and spent the night in the village of Chécy. She stayed there until the following afternoon, then set out for Orléans, reaching it when it was dark, at about eight o'clock. In full armor and mounted on a white horse, she rode at the right hand of Dunois, with her standard borne before her. She entered the town by the Burgundian Gate and was at once surrounded by a great and rejoicing crowd. A merchant of the town declared: "She was received with as much joy and enthusiasm by all, men and women, small and great, as if she had been an angel of God. For they hoped that through her they would be delivered from their enemies."

Nearly everyone carried a blazing torch, and the smoky light glinted from Joan's armor and lit up her dark, eager face. In the excitement, a torch was thrust too near her standard and set it on fire. Joan spurred her horse up to it and beat out the flame. Then she went to the church of the Sainte-Croix and gave thanks for her safe arrival. She was lodged at the house of Jacques Boucher, a wealthy man and the Duke of Orléans' treasurer. There her armor was taken off and she ate a few bits of bread dipped in wine and water offered to her in a silver cup. Then she went to bed, sharing it with Charlotte, her host's daughter, a child of nine.

The next day the military leaders held a council of war in Jacques Boucher's house. Outside in the streets the town's militiamen were parading up and down, clamoring for Joan to lead them against the enemy. Several hotheads among the leaders were only too willing to take part in such an excursion, but Dunois decided against it and tempers ran high—particularly Joan's. A close colleague of Dunois, Jean de Gamache, had no faith in Joan, and when it seemed at one point that her view was going to win the day he burst out with: "Since you chose to follow the counsel of a low-born wench rather than that of a knight of my birth, I lower my banner and will fight as a humble squire, though I should prefer to have a nobleman as master rather than a woman of no account." Dunois at once had to make the peace between them and persuaded them to a reluctant embrace. It was finally decided that Dunois should return to Blois and escort the army back to Orléans. But the day was not spent wholly in talk. A little later La Hire and Florent d'Illiers, another captain, with some of their own soldiers and a body of militiamen, sallied out from the walls, launched an attack on the English immediately north of the town, and drove them back into the fort of St. Pouair. There the English rallied and beat off the attack. A few men on both sides were killed and more were wounded— all to no purpose.

Joan knew nothing of this skirmish until it was over. In the afternoon she went out beyond the walls and on to a bridge across the river, from which she was within hailing distance of the English. She shouted to them, "In the name of God surrender and I will grant you your lives." An English captain, Sir William Glasdale, and his men hurled insults at her, calling her a whore, a cow-girl, and promising to burn her if they caught her. They called the French who were with her "unbelieving pimps."

The next morning she and La Hire and a few soldiers rode

out for a short way with Dunois and those who were returning to Blois. Dunois and his party had to pass between two of the English forts, yet as Joan's squire reported: "Notwithstanding the great power and numbers of the English army, thanks be to God, my lord Dunois and I got through with all our men and safely went our way. And the Maid and her men regained the town in equal safety." Here again we see the astonishing inertia of the English. They could fairly easily have killed or captured both Dunois and Joan, but not one English soldier emerged from his strongpoint. Dunois was away for four days. The English knew he had gone to Blois to bring back an army. Meanwhile Orléans lay before them, without its ablest soldier and as weak as it would ever be. And formidable reinforcements were being summoned. It was the moment to strike with every ounce of their strength. Yet they did nothing. To quote Hume again: "The English felt their courage daunted and overwhelmed, and thence inferred a divine vengeance hanging over them. The French drew the same inference from an inactivity so new and unexpected. Every circumstance was now reversed in the opinions of men, on which all depends. The spirit resulting from a long course of uninterrupted success was on a sudden transferred from the victors to the vanquished."

During the days of waiting for Dunois' return, Joan went about the town and showed herself to all its people. "One day," a witness reported, "a great lord was cursing and blaspheming God in a shameful manner in the street. Joan heard him, immediately went up to him, grasped him by the shoulder, and said, 'How dare you blaspheme our Lord and Master? In God's name, you will withdraw your words before I take another step.' And the lord repented and begged to be forgiven." She also made another appeal to the English and was answered by the same abuse. On May 3, the feast of the Finding of the Holy Cross, Joan rode to the cathedral behind the Blessed Sacrament, and those near her saw tears pouring down her face. That evening the watchmen on the tower of the cathedral reported that the relieving army from Blois could be seen on the horizon and that it was moving along the north bank of the Loire, the route which Joan had wanted the troops she accompanied to use.

Early next morning Joan and some five hundred men rode out to meet the army. Once again, both her small force and that led by Dunois were unmolested by the English. At about ten o'clock that morning she was eating her usual meal—a few crusts of bread dipped in wine and water—when Dunois called on her. He told her that Sir John Fastolf, the English leader who had been victorious in the Battle of the Herrings, was approaching the city with supplies and men. Joan's squire, Jean d'Aulon, reports: "The Maid seemed highly delighted with this news and said to my lord Dunois: 'Bastard, Bastard, in the name of God I command you to let me know the moment you hear that Fastolf is near. For if he gets through without my knowing it, I swear to you that I will have your head off!' To which my lord Dunois answered that he did not doubt it and that he would not fail to let her know." Joan then went to her room to rest. She lay down on the bed with her hostess, and Jean d'Aulon stretched himself out on a couch in the same room.

There was peace for about an hour. Jean d'Aulon dropped off into a deep sleep and the two women dozed. Then bedlam broke out. Joan leaped from her bed with a great shout—Jean d'Aulon complains, "She woke me with the great noise she made"—and cried, "In God's name, my voices have told me that I must attack the English, but I don't know whether to attack them in their forts or go to deal with Fastolf, who is on his way with supplies."

Meanwhile, crowds of people were shouting in the street outside, crying that the English were slaughtering the French. Her confessor, Jean Pasquerel, and several other priests arrived and went up to her. By then she was shouting, "Where are those who should arm me? The blood of our people is staining the ground. In God's name, this is ill done. Why did no one waken me? Our soldiers are hard pressed before one of the enemy's forts. My arms! Bring me my arms and my horse!" Still half asleep, Jean d'Aulon rolled off his couch and began arming Joan, who remained in a state of great agitation. The moment he had finished, she raced down the stairs. There she saw her page, Louis de Coutes, and burst out at him, "You wretched boy! You did not tell me the blood of Frenchmen was being shed!" She ordered him to fetch her horse, remembered she had forgotten her personal standard, gave a great shout for it, and caught it as it was dropped to her by Jean d'Aulon from an upstairs window. Her horse arrived. She mounted and rode off at such speed that her horse's shoes struck showers of sparks from the cobbles. She made for the Burgundian Gate.

What exactly was happening? We must look at the plan of the town. A large body of French troops had sallied out of the Gate, advanced eastward, and attacked the only English fort on the east of the town, the Bastille St. Loup. The chronicles of the time leave much unexplained about this episode. Was it a sudden, unpremeditated attack? Is that why Joan knew nothing about it? Or was an attack planned as a diversion under cover of which more supplies could come down the river to the town? If it was, why was Joan not told? Did Dunois and his companions regard the affair as a small-scale skirmish, too unimportant an affair in which to involve Joan? We shall never know.

D'Aulon dashed after Joan and caught up with her at the Burgundian Gate. He says: "When we came there, we saw one of the townsmen being carried in. He was badly wounded, and the Maid asked the men carrying him who he was. When they told her he was a Frenchman, she said, 'I can never see French blood without my hair standing on end.'" They passed through the Gate and rode on to the fields to St. Loup, which they found under rather desultory attack by some fifteen hundred Frenchmen. Three hundred Englishmen were inside the fort. They were defending it ably and, as was usual in medieval warfare, were having the better of the argument merely because they were the defenders.

Joan's arrival transformed the situation. Clasping her standard, she rallied the French, who launched an immediate all-out assault on the fort and stormed it. At least a hundred and fourteen of the English were killed. The fort had been built around a church. Some of the English troops fled into the church and clothed themselves in priests' vestments. The French, of course, saw through the hurriedly assumed disguise and were going to cut them down, but Joan at once intervened. "Churchmen must be spared," she declared, and had them—forty in all—taken safely back to Orléans. The fortifications were burned to the ground. The whole business took only three hours, and two Frenchmen were killed. A small affair, we think, one hardly worth recording. Yet it meant that Orléans was now open to the east and, much more important, that the terrible English had at last been defeated and smoked out of one of their key forts. The legend of their invincibility was destroyed.

It was the first time that Joan had seen what fighting meant. She wept because the English had died without, in all probability, having been confessed. She herself confessed to her chaplain before she left the conquered fort and made him issue this order to the French: "Confess your sins and thank God for the victory. If you do not, the Maid will cease to help you and will leave you." That night, the chronicles recount, "thanks were given to God in every church. There were hymns and prayers and the bells rang out. The English could hear them. In that fight they had been greatly reduced in strength and also in courage."

The next day, May 5, was the Feast of the Ascension, and Joan gave orders that there should be no fighting. She confessed again and received the Blessed Sacrament. She also ordered that no one should leave the town on the following day to take part in any fighting unless he had been to confession. She declared, too, that all the women camp followers should be sent packing. It was, she said, because of such sins that the war had been going so badly for the French. She was obeyed.

The leaders held a council of war in the house where Joan was staying and did not think it necessary to invite her to be present. They decided that they would next day attack the fort of St. Laurent, an English stronghold on the north bank of the river, west of the town. This attack was to be a feint; their main thrust was to be across the river in an effort to take the English forts on the southern bank. With their plan decided, they sent for Joan, and Dunois told her they were going to attack the fort of St. Laurent. She was not deceived. Walking up and down the room with great strides, she accused them of keeping her in the dark. "Tell me what you have really decided," she cried. "I could keep a far greater secret than that." Dunois then told her the truth: "Joan, you must not be angry. We can't tell you everything at once. We are indeed going to attack the fort of St. Laurent, but if the English along the south of the river should go to the assistance of that fort we shall cross the river and attack the forts there. We believe this is a good and profitable plan." Joan's anger left her. She agreed that the plan was good and that it should be carried out.

Then she made a final appeal to the English. She dictated this letter to Brother Pasquerel: "You men of England, who have no right to be here in the kingdom of France, the King of Heaven commands you through me, Joan the Maid, to leave your forts and return to your own country. If you will not, I will make a noise such as will never be forgotten. I write to you for the third and last time. I shall write no more." It was signed: "Jesus-Maria. Joan the Maid." She took it to the end of the broken bridge across the Loire, had it fastened to an arrow and shot across to the English, shouting as it flew through the air, "Read! A message for you!" The English read it and shouted back, "Ah! News from the French whore!" Joan wept.

This business of a council of war making its plans without Joan shows the peculiarity of her position. She was never, at any time in her short career, the leader of the army. The towns-people of Orléans and the ordinary soldier obeyed her implicitly and would have followed her anywhere. But most of the leaders—hard, practical men—treated her rather as a divine mascot. Dunois himself did not, but his authority was not absolute. He had to consult his fellow commanders and they, to the very end, could not get out of their minds the fact that Joan was very young and a girl, wholly without experience in war. As time went on, they were forced to realize the remarkable effect she had on the courage and determination of the troops, but they were never able to admit that in matters of tactics and strategy she showed better judgment and more sense. It is true that she had the wholehearted support of the King and so, in theory, should have been consulted about every move in the war. But the favor of the King did not mean that Joan became his representative in the field. The hierarchy of command was not really disturbed. Without her, the defeats of the French would have continued until they were ended by final and irrevocable disaster, but it was not the orders she gave which turned defeat into victory, for she was not empowered to give any orders. She could only urge and plead and sway the military, both leaders and troops, by the astonishing force of her personality, a force given her by God.

We left Joan in tears at the insults shouted at her by the English. She went to bed early that night and rose the next morning, May 6, at dawn. She made her confession and heard Mass. The day did not go as it had been planned by the captains, though the result of the day's actions was the same.

There was no attack made against the St. Laurent fort west of the town, because the armed citizens, the militia bands, chose otherwise. They thronged to the Burgundian Gate, which was shut and guarded by soldiers commanded by a veteran captain, the Sire de Gaucourt. He refused to open it, so word was sent to Joan. She rode to the Gate at once and stormed at de Gaucourt, "You are a wicked man not to open the Gate! But, whether you wish it or not, they will go out and will give as good an account of themselves as they did the other day." The citizens pressed forward in an ugly mood. De Gaucourt hastily gave orders for the Gate to be opened and declared, "I will be your captain."

For the moment Joan stayed behind as the armed mob swept

out. They went down to the river, commandeered some boats, and rowed over to the Ile-aux-Toiles, an island very close to the southern bank. They built a short bridge of boats to link the island to this bank and marched over it. When they approached the first English fort, that of St.-Jean-le-Blanc, they found it deserted. So they marched on to the next, Les Augustins, which covered the approaches to the key English stronghold, Les Tourelles—the position and importance of which I shall deal with shortly. Here matters were very different. The English emerged from behind their fortifications and set about the French with something of their old vigor. They were more than a match for the citizen-soldiers and began to drive them back. Just when it seemed that their retreat was going to end in rout and massacre, the regular French forces arrived from across the river with Joan and La Hire at their head. These two mounted their horses, couched their lances, and charged. The rest followed and drove the English back into their fort. It was not long before the fort was stormed. Many of the English escaped and took refuge in the Tourelles; many were killed and a few made prisoners. Joan had dismounted during the hand-to-hand fighting and was wounded in the foot when she trod on one of the spiked metal balls which were scattered about the ground to disable the horses of the knights. The day had exhausted her and, though she usually fasted on Fridays, she ate when she got back to the town. Her confessor tells what happened then:

"After dinner a valiant and famous knight came to visit her. He told Joan that the King's captains and leaders had held counsel together, that they saw how inferior in numbers they were to the English, and that they knew it was by God's special grace that they had won the successes they had. Seeing that the

town is well stocked with provisions, we shall be very likely
to hold until the King sends more aid, and the council do not
think it necessary for the soldiers to sally forth tomorrow. Joan
replied, 'You have been to your council and I to mine. And
believe me, the counsel of the Lord will hold good and will
be accomplished, while your counsel will perish.' Then she
turned to me, who was beside her, and said, 'Get up earlier
tomorrow, earlier even than you did today, and do your best.
Keep near me all the time, for I shall have much to do tomorrow, more than I have ever had, and the blood will flow from
my body above my breast.' "

Jean Pasquerel rose very early next morning—the morning
of Saturday, May 7, 1429. More than five hundred years have
gone by since then, yet the people of Orléans have not forgotten
that day, and each year it is marked by gay and splendid ceremonies, by Masses, by processions, by dancing in the streets,
and by the rush of soaring rockets whose falling dazzle of stars is
reflected in the placid waters of the Loire. Pasquerel said Mass
and gave Joan Holy Communion, and she was ready to begin
the day which was to restore the unity of France and start her
on her path to greatness among the nations.

The day is known as "the day of the Tourelles." The only
bridge from Orléans to the south bank of the Loire joined the
town to an island—the Ile St. Antoine—about a quarter of the
way across the water, and then continued across a broad stretch
of the river until it reached the south bank. On it, just before
it touched the bank, stood Les Tourelles, a small but massively
built fortress with four turrets. It was garrisoned with about
six hundred English troops. Between the Ile St. Antoine and
the Tourelles, part of the bridge had been destroyed. On the
south bank, and jutting into the river, an outwork had been

built—an embankment with high walls. From it the defenders of the Tourelles could pour down arrows upon any force trying to approach the fort. The Tourelles was linked by a drawbridge to that end of the outwork which stood out into the river.

The decision of the military council that there were to be no sallies from the town that day had reached the civil leaders. They went straight to Joan and said, "We have consulted together and we have come to beg you to fulfill the mission given you by God and the King." Her answer was, "In God's name, that I will do," and, astride her horse, she cried, "Let those who love me follow me!" As she rode away from the house where she had been staying she promised her host, the treasurer, "Tonight we shall return by the bridge."

Dunois, the marshals, the counts, the lord of this, and the lord of that, saw that they could not stand against this demand for action from the townsfolk, so once again Joan had her way, not because she changed their plans by any argument, but because the ordinary people had unbounded faith in her and insisted that she should be obeyed.

The attack began very early in the day. It was launched against the outwork protecting the Tourelles. The French brought great faggots of wood to fill in the ditch which had been dug all along its base and then tried to scale it with ladders. Many reached the top, only to be beaten off and hurled down by the English defenders. Noon came. Some of the French were dead, some wounded, but the outwork and its soldiers were unscathed. So, in the civilized manner of that day, everyone stopped fighting and took an hour off to eat. At the end of the hour's break Joan picked up a ladder and reared it against the side of the outwork, but she had no sooner put her foot on the first rung than she was struck by an arrow which drove six inches into her, above her right breast. She fell and was carried out of range, weeping with pain and shock. Soldiers crowded round her and wanted to use charms to heal her, but she refused their help, saying, "I would rather die than do what I know to be a sin or to be against the law of God." She declared, "I know that I must die, but I do not know when or how or where or at what hour. If I can be healed now without sin, I am willing to be cured." So the upper part of her armor was taken off and she pulled the arrow out herself. Olive oil and lard were put on the wound; she made her confession to Brother Pasquerel and returned to the fighting.

There nothing had changed. The French still attacked and the English still beat them off. The afternoon was wearing on, and it would not be long before night fell. Dunois thought there was no longer any chance of capturing the outwork that day and decided to withdraw his forces within the walls of the town. The retreat was sounded. Joan, hearing the trumpets, rushed to Dunois and begged him not to desert the field for a little longer. "In God's name," she assured him, "it will not be long now before you take the fort." She told the soldiers, "Rest a little and eat and drink." She herself rode off to a vineyard a little distance away and prayed there for about ten minutes. Dusk was gathering when she came back.

Joan's standard was carried by a soldier nicknamed the Basque. D'Aulon, Joan's squire, asked him if he would follow him to the base of the outwork. The Basque agreed, and d'Aulon scrambled down into the ditch and, crouching with his shield held over his head, advanced toward the outwork. The Basque followed him down and, when Joan reappeared on the scene, she saw her standard disappearing into the hollow. She raced forward and managed to grab it by its tail, shouting,

"My standard! My standard!" The Basque, not realizing what was happening, held fast to the pole, and in the half-light the French forces saw the standard violently agitated, took its movements as a signal, and began to move forward again. The Basque tore the standard from Joan's grasp and ran toward the outwork's wall. At once Joan shouted, "Wait till my standard touches the wall!" A moment later the tail of the standard brushed the wall and, like men possessed, the French surged forward—great nobles, knights, ordinary soldiers, and the armed citizens of the town. It was said they looked "like a flock of birds descending on a hedge." In an irresistible tide they swept forward across the ditch and up the wall.

The English were bewildered and did nothing for a moment or two. Their hesitation, brief though it was, was fatal. By the time they started to fight they were overwhelmed. But they kept their heads and began a fighting retreat to what they imagined was the absolute safety of the Tourelles.

Meanwhile, a crowd of armed French had left Orléans by the Bridge Gate and swarmed on to the broken bridge leading to the Tourelles. When they reached the gap in the bridge, they managed to fling a plank across it and batter down the palisades protecting the Tourelles from that side. Most of the English soldiers had got back into the fortress and now found themselves attacked from the rear. Their leaders were still trying to stem the French onslaught from the outwork but were pressed steadily back. Behind them was the wooden drawbridge linking the outwork to the Tourelles. Once across it, they could hope for a moment's respite. But early that day the people of Orléans had secured a large barge, loaded it with tar, gallons of olive oil, wood, tow, resin, and sulphur, and had managed to fasten it beneath this wooden drawbridge. There, very late in the fighting, it was lit, and as night came its smoky glare enveloped the bridge and its flames ate through the planking, so that as the heavily armored English leaders stepped on it the whole structure collapsed and between thirty and forty English lords and captains were plunged into the Loire and drowned. One of them was Glasdale, who had so often hurled insults at Joan. Probably the last words he heard were those shouted at him by Joan as she saw him nearing the fatal bridge: "Glacidas! Glacidas! [None of the French ever seemed able to pronounce his name.] Surrender to the King of Heaven! You called me a whore, but I have great pity for your soul and the souls of your men."

Within the Tourelles bitter fighting continued, but as French reinforcements poured in from the town the English were overwhelmed and slaughtered. Scarcely any prisoners were taken. As Joan had prophesied early that morning, the victorious French marched back into Orléans across the bridge, back to a town ablaze with torches and noisy with pealing bells and thousands of voices chanting the *Te Deum laudamus*. Dunois reported: "And Joan was taken to her lodging so that her wound might be dressed. When the surgeon had finished, she had her supper, eating four or five toasts soaked in wine and water. She had taken no other food or drink all that day."

It was a day that began the ending of English power in France.

The next morning was Sunday, May 8, the feast of the Apparition of St. Michael. The watchman on the western towers of Orléans saw the English pour out of the forts they still held and line up in battle order. They were still very numerous and looked still formidable. Joan was told of their movements and persuaded Dunois to assemble the French troops outside the walls, so that the two armies faced each other. The French outnumbered the English and were eager to attack, spurred on by their great victory of the preceding day. But the English were in the same formation as that adopted at Agincourt. They would not collapse when pushed. Some of the French soldiers asked Joan if they could fight. Her answer was, "We must hear Mass." And Mass was celebrated on a portable altar. She then said, "In honor of Sunday, this holy day, stay your hands, for that is God's will. If the English want to march away, you must do nothing to prevent them. But if they attack you, then defend yourselves boldly. And don't be afraid, for you will overcome them." A second Mass was celebrated. Toward its end, the English began to move. When Joan was told, she asked, "Are they facing this way?" They were not. "Then," she said, "they are leaving. Let them go and let us thank God. It is not His will that we should pursue them. You will get them another time."

One of Joan's biographers has written: "Such episodes as her having allowed the English army to retreat after the defeat at Orléans must be reckoned among the mistakes she made. The fact that the day was Sunday was more important to her than the fact that she then held the English in her power. Because of the Sabbath, she allowed them to escape. One can only draw the conclusion that, on this occasion at least, she was no great commander, but an inspired sentimentalist." No explanation is given as to why it should be sentimental to keep Sunday holy and free of bloodshed. But that apart, this comment shows a complete lack of understanding of the art of war. The English were not a beaten army. Their loss of the Tourelles meant that they had lost Orléans, and in the long run that was fatal to them, but for the moment it was merely the loss of a single town. As they stood in the meadows outside Orléans on that Sunday morning, they were still extremely dangerous, and Joan would have been rash and incompetent had she engaged in a pitched battle with them. An hour's fighting might have seen the destruction of the French, with the town an easy prize for the victorious English. It is a sound maxim in war that you pursue a beaten enemy and give him no time to re-form or regroup. But this English army was not beaten. It had lost six hundred men and one fort, but its main forces had never been engaged. So Joan's decision was as sensible as it was Christian.

So the English left Orléans, never to come back to it again except as tourists. They went away two hundred and nine days after they arrived before its walls and nine days after Joan rode in. The Duke of Bedford declared, "This mischief was largely caused by the fear the soldiers had of a disciple and limb of the fiend, known as the Maid, who used enchantments and sorcery against them."

5. The Capture

J OAN ALSO left Orléans. She went to Blois and then on to Tours. The King was still at Chinon, but he came to Tours and Joan rode a little way out of the town to meet him. She pulled off her cap and bowed low over her horse. Charles took off his hat, raised her face, and kissed her. They were together in Tours for ten days and then moved to Loches, another of the great châteaux so beloved by Charles. Throughout this time Joan gave the King little peace. She urged him to go to Rheims to be crowned. Dunois says: "She gave as her reason for this advice that, once he was crowned and anointed, the power of his enemies would decline continually until finally they would be powerless to harm either him or his kingdom."

Charles did not act quickly enough for her, but it is unfair to charge him with irresolution after the relief of Orléans. It is plain that Joan's triumph there had swept away any possible doubts he may have had about her, but with the best will in the world he could not act at the speed demanded by Joan. He could not go to Rheims through territory of which much was held by the English without the most careful planning and more fighting. Joan's impatience grew.

At Loches, the King was one day holding council with two or three intimates. They were talking in one of those wooden rooms which were built within the great hall of a castle to afford some privacy. Joan knocked on the door, entered, and fell on her knees before the King and burst out with, "Noble Dauphin, do not talk and debate so much, but come quickly to Rheims to be rightfully crowned." One of the lords asked her, "Is it your counselors who tell you to say this?" She said, "Yes, and they speak urgently about it." The lord then asked her if she would tell him how her counselors gave their messages. The King also asked her, "Joan, please tell him in the presense of us all here." She blushed and said, "When I am angry because God's words, spoken by me, are not believed or acted upon, I go apart and pray to Him and tell Him that no one has faith in what I say. And after I have prayed I hear a voice which says, 'Go forward, child of God, go forward, go forward and I will help you.' I am overwhelmed with joy and wish I could listen to that voice forever." Dunois was present and he says, "As she told us this, her eyes were raised to heaven and she seemed in ecstasy."

Very soon after this the King decided to march on Rheims, but he and his advisers considered it was essential before moving north to clear the English from the positions they still held on the banks of the Loire. The Duke of Alençon was made lieutenant general of the royal army. On June 6, Joan and the advance guard set off from Selles-en-Berry. A spectator has recorded the scene: "She was in her plain armor, with her head bare, and she held a small ax. The horse was a big black charger and was so lively that she couldn't mount it. So she said, 'Lead him to the cross,' which stood at the side of the road near the church. Once he was there, the horse stood as still as if he were bound. She mounted him, turned to the church porch and said, in her clear woman's voice, 'You priests and you other people, go in procession and pray to God.' She turned her horse's head to the road and cried, 'Forward! Forward!' Her page rode before her, carrying her furled banner."

There were three English strongholds on the Loire: the two towns of Meung and Beaugency, both to the west of

Orléans, and the town of Jargeau, some twelve miles to the east. Jargeau was held by the Earl of Suffolk, and it was known that Sir John Fastolf, the able and ruthless English commander, was on his way to it from Paris at the head of two thousand men. It was decided to attack and take Jargeau before Fastolf reached it.

The French spent two nights in Orléans on the way, and the townspeople, with the memory of their deliverance fresh in their minds, gave Joan a rapturous reception. When the French marched out on the road to Jargeau, they numbered about five thousand. They slept in the woods the first night. It seems that there was some hesitancy, some timidity, some doubt among the leaders even though they were committed to the taking of Jargeau, for Joan had to tell them, "Do not be afraid, no matter how large is the English host, and do not hesitate to attack them, for it is God who directs this work. You can be very sure that if I were not convinced that God is with us, I would rather be herding sheep than suffer so much hardship and danger."

They continued their march next day and arrived within sight of the town in the late afternoon. Suffolk led his men out, there was a sharp skirmish, and the French began to fall back. Joan, her standard waving, plunged into the fighting and, as usual, the French rallied and drove the English back within their walls. That night Joan urged the English to surrender, "Yield this place to the King of Heaven and the Dauphin or you will suffer greatly." The invitation was ignored.

The assault on the town began at nine o'clock next morning. It was not a very strongly fortified place, but it was ringed by a moat which had to be filled with brushwood under the arrows of the English. The job was done at last and Joan turned to Alençon: "Forward, my Duke, and storm the walls!" He seemed to hesitate. Joan laughed and said, "Surely you are not afraid! Don't you remember that I promised your wife to send you home to her safe and sound?" So he gave the order for the general assault. Joan stayed by his side and after a few moments pointed out a piece of artillery mounted on the wall in front of him. "Move to one side," she told Alençon, "or that thing will most certainly kill you." He obeyed and moved a few yards to the right. A young nobleman from Angers took his place, and a stone ball from the cannon smashed him to the ground and killed him. "At which," confessed Alençon, "I was very much afraid and wondered greatly at the way the things she spoke of came to pass." After this incident he and Joan joined in the attack. Joan climbed up a ladder against the wall. One of the defenders hurled down a stone which landed on her steel cap and knocked her off the ladder. She staggered to her feet and shouted, "Up, comrades, up, up! Our Lord has doomed the English. They are ours, they are ours! So be of good cheer!" Within a minute or two the French were in the town and more than eleven hundred of the English defenders were being slaughtered. Their commander, the Earl of Suffolk, managed to surrender.

Joan and the Duke rode back to Orléans, whose citizens thanked them with speeches and, more sensibly, with wine —six casks to the Duke and four to Joan. She was also given a cloak and tunic in the colors of the Orléans family—red and green. One of Joan's harmless and attractive weaknesses was for pretty and striking clothes. She liked bright colors and rich materials and wore them with delight.

From Orléans, the French forces went out again. This time they marched downstream to Meung. There they seized only the bridge across the river and moved on to Beaugency, a much more important stronghold of the English. They, when the French arrived, withdrew into the castle which towered above the town. For the length of a day they were bombarded by mortars and cannon, and at midnight they offered to surrender the castle provided they were allowed to ride away. The French accepted this offer on condition the English swore not to fight again for the next ten days. This they did and so were allowed to depart. No one recounts if Joan had any part in this episode, though it is not unlikely, for, as we have seen, it was her habit always to offer the English the chance of surrendering before the final struggle began.

Meanwhile, Sir John Fastolf had learned of the fall of Jargeau, so he changed his line of march and headed toward Beaugency. He was joined by another English commander, Sir John Talbot, and his men. Their combined forces made up an army of about five thousand men. Then came the news that Beaugency had gone, news followed almost immediately by the sight of the standards and pennons of France, for the Duke of Alençon was cautiously exploring the country north of Beaugency to try to get news of the English and find out what they were up to.

Both armies were startled by this meeting. The French, it must be remembered, had never within living memory defeated the English in the open field, and though they were emboldened by their great triumph at Orléans and their lesser one at Beaugency, they showed no great enthusiasm at the prospect of a pitched battle. Alençon asked Joan's advice. She said, "Have you good spurs?" Amiable though he was, he does not seem to have had a very quick mind, and he thought she was suggesting they should retreat. She laughed. "No! The English won't be able to face your attack. They will be utterly defeated and will flee and you will need your spurs if you are to keep up with them." Alençon and his fellow captains were reassured. By now they were all convinced that Joan spoke with supernatural authority. If she said the English would be defeated, that was all there was to it and victory was assuredly theirs. But it was evening, and the battles of those days were, if possible, daylight affairs. The English sent the conventional heralds to the French with the conventional challenge for three French knights to meet three English knights in single combat. The French replied, "It grows late, so go and find lodging for the night. If God and Our Lady so desire, we shall come to grips with you tomorrow."

When morning came, however, the English were gone. They had lost their nerve and had begun to retreat northward to Janville, a town they still held. The country through which they marched was flat and well wooded—ideal territory for a retreating army to lose itself in. The French set out in pursuit. Joan gazed at the clouds in the sky and cried, "In God's name, we'll get them even if they hide in the clouds! Today our Dauphin will have his greatest victory. My voices have told me they will all be ours." About eighty men, who had the best horses, were sent forward to try to track down the English. They rode for more than ten miles without finding a trace of them. Then occurred one of those chances by which armies and even kingdoms have been lost. The French scouts startled a stag from a thicket. It went crashing away through the undergrowth and they heard the noise of its frightened progress grow fainter and fainter. It had almost died away when distant, excited shouts came from the direction the stag had taken. The beast had burst into the open and into full view of the rear guard covering the English retreat, and the soldiers, forgetting all caution, greeted it with the cries of the hunting field. Those cries were to cost them dearly. The French sent riders back to their main body of troops with the news that the English were found. They too forgot caution, and it was not long before the English knew they had been spotted.

Sir John Talbot, with five hundred archers, at once prepared for action. They were about a mile from the little town of Patay, on a track with dense hedges on each side. The archers began driving in their pointed stakes, but before they could assume their usual and deadly formation the French cavalry were upon and through them. They destroyed the English rear guard, charged on, and cut into the main force. There, too, they wrought great havoc. It was June 18, and the slaughter is known as the Battle of Patay. Nearly three thousand English were killed. Three Frenchmen died. Joan came late to the scene, but she was in time to see a Frenchman knock one of his prisoners on the head. She ran forward and held the dying man's head on her breast and tried to comfort him until a priest came and heard his confession.

She returned to Orléans the next day, and a day or two later saw the King at St. Benoit-sur-Loire. He said he was grieved at all the labor she was undergoing for his sake and suggested she should rest. She wept, probably because she was indeed weary and because the kindness of his words moved her, but she persisted in her demand that he should go to Rheims to be crowned. That was still her prime purpose and nothing could shake her from it.

Many of those who have written about St. Joan have sharply criticized her for this, saying she should have insisted that the French army march on Paris. They argue that, with Paris in his hands, the whole of France would have been the King's.

Because Joan insisted that his coronation should come first, she is attacked as a dreamer, a visionary with no understanding of practical affairs, no sense of the realities of power. I find this attitude incomprehensible. These writers produce a book about Joan solely because she was a visionary, solely because she achieved what she did as a result of being completely obedient to her heavenly voices and ignoring the earthly voices counseling prudence and common sense. Unless she had been true to her voices she would have been nothing, yet every now and then her biographers have a fit of testiness when they see her standing firm and refusing to be swayed by the pleadings of expediency. They object, in fact, to Joan behaving like St. Joan. But in this matter of the coronation she was obeying both her voices and the dictates of practical politics.

To argue that the proper course was to have tried to take Paris before the King was crowned is to reveal a startling ignorance of the Middle Ages in general and of medieval France in particular. When a monarch died, his lawful heir immediately became the ruler of the kingdom—"the king is dead, long live the king." When a king is the real effective force in the state, there can be no gap between his death and the assumption of full power by his successor. To allow such a gap is to ask for rebellion and anarchy. But, in the eyes of his subjects, no king was fully king until his coronation, for a king was not merely a political figure. Within his own sphere, he was God's regent and at the coronation ceremony he pledged himself to God and was accepted by God and consecrated by His priests. He only entered into the fullness of his kingship with this consecration. Not one of Joan's fellow citizens would ever have considered Charles as true King until his crowning. Those Frenchmen loyal to his cause accepted him as the lawful heir to the throne of France, the man who had the right to be crowned, but in their eyes he had not stepped over that mystic line which separated him from his subjects and placed him in a wholly different category of human beings. That irrevocable step could be taken only in the Cathedral of Rheims.

Some medieval kings were singularly unsavory specimens, more concerned with satisfying their lust for power than with fulfilling their role of God's regent, but their activities do nothing to invalidate the theory of kingship to which the whole Christian world subscribed. In France, supreme importance was attached to a thing called *La Sainte-Ampoule,* a small glass phial which contained a few drops of coagulated oil. When Clovis, King of the Franks, married a Christian wife and became a Christian himself, a dove descended carrying this phial in its beak and, with the oil it held, St. Rémy anointed the first Christian King of France as he was baptized. The amount of oil never grew less, though every succeeding King had been anointed with it. That was the legend and it is probably quite untrue. But what is undoubtedly true is that this phial had existed from the end of the fifth century and that the oil inside it, whether miraculously renewed or topped by human hands, was considered an absolutely essential element in the coronation of a king of France. The *Sainte-Ampoule* was kept in the Abbey of St. Rémy in Rheims. Only once was it ever allowed to leave the town: when Louis XI was dying in 1483, he was given permission by the Pope to have it brought to his bedside to comfort him. When the "grotesque tragedy" of the Revolution broke over France, one of the revolutionary deputies deliberately smashed the phial, thus destroying his country's most venerable relic with that brutal callousness which is characteristic of revolutionaries of every age and country.

Charles was a devout Christian. He undoubtedly believed in the supernatural virtue of the oil of the *Sainte-Ampoule.* Anointed with it, he would feel a great weight of uncertainty roll off his soul. He would know himself to be truly King and so would every one of his subjects. And the enemies of his realm, the English, would feel uneasy. In that age, as in this, there was often a wide gulf between belief and practice, and no amount of oil poured out in Rheims could have persuaded the English to withdraw from France. Yet even Bedford, hard-bitten statesman though he was, realized that Charles's coronation would gravely worsen the English position. He twice urged that Henry VI, the child-king of England, should be sent to France so that he could be crowned at Rheims and thus have his title to the French throne made more respectable. So Joan's thrusting of Charles along the road to Rheims was a piece of sensible statecraft. It was thought to be so by her contemporaries, including the King himself. The only point in dispute between him and Joan in this matter was when he should go to Rheims. He, dilatory as always, could not see the need for desperate hurry. She told him, "I shall last but little more than a year, so see that you make good use of me during this time." She knew that her days were numbered and wanted unceasing haste so that she could accomplish all she had to do.

It was at last decided that she should have her way. The army assembled at Gien on the Loire and, accompanied by the King and Joan, began its march to Rheims. They entered Troyes and Châlons, and outside Rheims a deputation came to the King and offered its surrender. The coronation was fixed for the following day, July 17, 1429. It was a Sunday, for an old tradition declared that the King of France should be crowned on that day. Throughout the night, work went on to prepare the cathedral for the ceremony. Early in the morning, four great lords went to the Abbey of St. Rémy to escort the abbot bearing the *Sainte-Ampoule* to the church of St. Denis. Awaiting them there was the Archbishop of Rheims, who took the holy vessel and headed a great procession to the cathedral, where he placed the *Ampoule* upon the altar.

The sun glowed through the rich hues of the vast windows as the King, with Joan at his side, advanced down the nave. Joan carried her standard. When she was on trial for her life, she was asked why she bore her standard into the cathedral. She said, "It had flown over scenes of great peril, so it was right and proper that it should be honored then." It was a true coronation performed on that summer morning, but much was lacking. The crown of Charlemagne and his sword were in the hands of the English, as were the golden spurs of St. Louis and the Pontifical containing the order of the ceremony. When the herald summoned the twelve peers of France to stand before the altar, not one of the secular peers came forth. They had all deserted to the enemy long before. Other nobles, headed by the Duke of Alençon, stepped forward to take their place. Only three of the ecclesiastical peers were present. Charles swore that he would protect the Church, that he would not oppress his people with excessive taxation, and that he would govern with justice and mercy. The Archbishop then anointed him with the holy oil—on the head, on the shoulders, the breast, and the hands. As the oil touched his head and the Archbishop said, "With this holy oil, I anoint thee King, in the name of the Father, the Son, and the Holy Ghost," Charles became truly King. A crown was placed on his head, the trumpets sounded, and the crowd shouted in joyful acclamation.

Throughout the ceremony Joan stood at the side of the King.

A witness says: "When the Maid saw that the King was crowned, she knelt before him, clasped him around the knees and, with tears pouring down her face, said, 'Now the will of God is accomplished—that I should set Orléans free and bring you to this city of Rheims, so that you have a holy anointing and crowning and thus have it made plain that you are the true King to whom the realm of France should belong.'" Until that moment she had always referred to Charles as the Dauphin. It was the first time she had called him the King.

During her stay at Rheims she saw her father, who had made his way there to watch the crowning of his King. With him was another of her relatives, Durand Laxart, the man who had twice escorted her to Vaucouleurs. At Joan's request the King gave her father a document freeing the people of Domrémy from all taxes forever, a document which was honored until the Revolution.

The moment of the King's crowning at Rheims was, except for her death, the culmination of Joan's career. By human standards, the rest of her short life was one slow decline. The great, triumphant days were behind her. Her capture lay some ten months ahead. Until then, she is gradually edged out of the center of the picture and never again do we see her act with the same supreme confidence as that which marked her every move in the first five months with the King. She had freed Orléans and achieved the coronation of Charles. By so doing, she had given the French new heart. The way was clear for their final victory. But it seems as if God had decided that, as far as France was concerned, Joan's mission was over, though as St. Joan she would have a different and greater mission.

She had, after all, done what she had been sent to do. Dunois says: "She never affirmed anything except that she had been

sent to raise the siege of Orléans and help the oppressed people
in that town and the surrounding country, and to lead the King
to Rheims to be anointed." And, again reported by Dunois,
just after the coronation the Archbishop of Rheims asked her:
"Joan, where do you expect to die?" She replied, "Wherever
God pleases. For myself, I do not know the time or the place
of my death any more than you do. But please God that I may
now retire, lay down my arms, and go to serve my father and
mother and tend their sheep with my brothers and sisters, who
will all be pleased to have me with them again."

I do not propose to enter into a detailed examination of these
ten months. The events which do not directly involve Joan
are both dull and complicated, and the motives of the actors
in them are still unknown. Very briefly, though, the three
protagonists—Charles, the Duke of Burgundy, and the Duke
of Bedford—were all trying to gain their different ends by
intrigue rather than by fighting. Charles, by his coronation,
had gained immense prestige; Burgundy and Bedford were
still allies, but it was an alliance which showed increasing
strain. Neither wished to see the other too powerful, yet neither
desired to see Charles become King in fact, as he was legally, of
the whole of France. So short truces were signed, letters were
exchanged, promises were made and broken, insults were
bandied about, armies were advanced, then put into retreat,
one or two towns changed hands. All, in fact, was confusion,
with Charles gaining slightly, very slightly at the expense of
his two adversaries.

After his coronation Charles should have marched straight
on Paris. It could have been his in a week. He negotiated instead of marching. The negotiations achieved nothing, and
it was not until the end of August that the royal forces arrived

at St. Denis and within sight of the capital. An attack was made on the city on September 8. Later, at her trial, Joan said that her voices gave her no counsel on this occasion. She behaved with her usual courage, but the supernatural fire was lacking. The attack was launched at two points—against the St. Honoré and the St. Denis gates. These gates were protected by two ditches, of which the outer one was dry and the inner one full of water and about sixty feet across. We have a description of Joan standing on its bank and testing the depth of the water with a lance. An arrow hit her in the thigh. Her standard-bearer got an arrow through the foot. He raised the visor of his helmet, and a third arrow, straight between the eyes, killed him. Great efforts were made to fill the ditch with faggots and brushwood, but by nightfall it had not proved possible to place a single scaling ladder against the walls. Work should have gone on under cover of darkness. Instead, the attack was called off by order of the King.

Next day, preparations were made to continue the assault, with Joan urging Alençon not to pause until Paris was theirs and saying she would not leave until they were victorious. But Charles again intervened, sending two nobles to order them to return to St. Denis and join him there. Charles was not mad, though it may appear so from his behavior here. Unknown to Joan, he was receiving assurances from the Duke of Burgundy that Paris would be surrendered to him before long. It was foolish of Charles to trust Burgundy, a man of great ability but lacking all scruples and ready to utter any lie if he thought it would serve his purpose. That purpose was always the same: to increase the power of Burgundy. Yet these assurances gave Charles a reason for not pressing the attack on Paris, and although it was not a very good reason it does at least let us see that he was not behaving like a lunatic. He was, too, a humane man and detested unnecessary bloodshed. If there was a chance that Paris could be his without fighting, he would not fight. In the end there was no battle for Paris, but his refusal to support Joan at this time means that seven years were to pass before he entered his capital.

Joan laid her armor at the foot of Our Lady's statue in the cathedral of St. Denis and moved southward, away from Paris, with the King. On September 21 the royal party arrived at Gien and the army was disbanded. The Duke of Alençon returned to his estate of Beaumont-sur-Oise. Joan had promised his wife that she would send him home to her safe and sound, and no harm had come to him. He asked that Joan be allowed to go with him to help him reconquer his duchy, which was held by the English, but the King and his advisers would not let her go. She "remained with the King, saddened greatly by the departure of the Duke, for she loved him dearly and would do for him what she would do for no one else." Dunois and La Hire also left the court, and nothing more is heard of the young men who escorted her from Vaucouleurs to Chinon.

The King moved to Bourges, and there Joan lodged for three weeks in the home of the Receiver General. His wife was Marguerite La Touroulde, and Joan shared her bed. Marguerite has this to say of her guest: "She behaved like an honest and Christian woman. She went to confession very often, loved to hear Mass, and often asked me to go to Matins—which I did and took her with me several times. Someone once said to Joan that it was very natural for her not to mind fighting, as she knew she would not be killed. But Joan said she had no more assurance of her safety than had anyone else in the fight. She had a horror of gambling with dice. She was very simple and ignorant and I consider the only thing she knew anything about was the art of war. She could ride a horse and wield a lance as well as the finest soldier, and the soldiers themselves were astonished at her skill. I remember some women coming to the house while Joan was living there. They brought rosaries and other holy objects for her to touch. She burst out laughing and said to me, 'You touch them! Your touch is just as good as mine.' She was very generous in almsgiving and was always giving money to the needy. She said she had been sent to comfort the poor and destitute."

After Bourges, the court wandered from one château to another, with Joan always in attendance. It was then decided that two small places in the hands of the Burgundians should be taken. One of them was St. Pierre-le-Moutier, south of Nevers. The other, north of Nevers, was La Charité. At St. Pierre we see Joan for the last time successfully exercising her power over men in battle. At the end of October she and a small hurriedly gathered army were outside the walls of St. Pierre. After a short siege they tried to storm the town but were easily beaten off, and the whole investment of the place was about to be abandoned. Jean d'Aulon, Joan's squire, was present, hobbling about on crutches, because at the beginning of the siege an arrow had pierced his heel. As the French began to retreat, he saw no sign of Joan. He had himself put on a horse and rode back toward the walls. He found her and a few soldiers standing before the moat. He says: "I asked her what she was doing there and why she had not retreated with the rest. She swept off her helmet and cried, 'I am not alone. With me I have fifty thousand of my own company and I shall not budge until I have taken the town.'" D'Aulon, a prosaic, matter-of-fact man with never a thought about spiritual hosts, continues: "At that moment, whatever she might say, she had no more than four or five men with her. I am absolutely certain of that and so are several others who were there and saw her. So I told her to come away and join the retreat." She ordered him to send for bundles of brushwood to throw in the moat and form a bridge across it, then shouted the same command at the top of her voice, "Faggots, everybody, faggots so that we can make a bridge!" D'Aulon says: "And they were brought at once and thrown into position. Our men launched a new attack and the town was carried by assault. I was astonished."

Things did not go like this when the French attacked La Charité a month later. The town held out and Joan and her forces had to withdraw.

At Christmas, the King ennobled Joan, together with her parents, her brothers and sisters and all their descendants. He declared he did this to show his gratitude for "the countless and manifest signs of God's grace which have been bestowed on us because of the intervention of our dear and well-beloved Maid, Joan of Arc." A few days later the people of Orléans gave Joan a great banquet. Hares, capons, partridges, pheasants, and much wine were provided and, to cap the feast, Joan was presented with a house in the town. One of the pleasantest things in Joan's career is the quick and unfailing gratitude always shown her by the citizens of Orléans. They had, it is true, a good deal to be grateful for, but, human nature being what it is, one is accustomed to find that gratitude is an emotion which quickly dies.

At this time an uneasy truce governed the relations between the King and the Duke of Burgundy. From time to time it was broken in a small way by both parties, but gradually the Duke began to break it more thoroughly. There was news, too, that the English had landed more men at Calais. Joan told the King, "You will find no peace except at the point of the lance," and he realized she was right. The people of Rheims grew frightened that they would be the first target of the English and the Burgundians when the fighting flared up again, and they wrote of their fears to Joan. She replied with a letter in which there is all her old dash and confidence: "My beloved friends: Joan the Maid, who longs to see you again, has received the letter in which you say you are afraid of being besieged. You can be quite sure this will not happen if I can get at the enemy quickly. But if I cannot and they do appear, shut your gates and I shall soon be with you. And I will make them take to their heels and the siege will be raised almost before it has begun. Only remain true and loyal and may God keep you."

At the end of March a French force was sent northward from the Loire and Joan went with it. In Holy Week it appeared outside Melun, which at once rose in revolt and drove out the Burgundians. It was at this town that Joan learned how little time was left to her. Her voices said, "Joan, you will be captured before the feast of St. John. But do not be afraid. God will help you." This date was June 24, less than ten weeks ahead. She did not tell the soldiers of this, but henceforth she deferred to their leaders in military matters.

From Melun she and the soldiers moved north again to Lagny-sur-Marne, a town loyal to the King. They stayed there a day or two before continuing on to Senlis and then to Compiègne. This last town was a big, strong fortress and intensely hostile to England and to Burgundy. During the truce between Charles and the Duke, the Duke had proposed that

Compiègne be handed over to him as a hostage to ensure the keeping of the truce. Charles had foolishly agreed. It is hard—or, rather, it is impossible—to see why, as the town stood almost at the confluence of two rivers, the Aisne and the Oise, and stood astride the road to Paris from the north. But neither the commander of Compiègne nor its citizens, devoted though they were to the King, were prepared to obey him to the extent of handing themselves over to the Duke of Burgundy. They decided to remain a French town. When the farcical truce came to its official end, the Duke decided to take what he had been unable to get as a gift. He began by besieging Choisy, a small town a little way up the Aisne.

Joan planned to relieve Choisy. To do this, she had to cross the Aisne at Soissons. But the governor of Soissons, wavering in his loyalty to the King, refused to let her pass. The troops she led numbered about fifteen hundred, and at this check most of them deserted, leaving her with some two hundred and fifty men. Denied entrance to Soissons, she anounced, "I am now going to pay another visit to my good friends in Compiègne," and at the head of her small company she rode through the forest back to Compiègne. The governor of the town was Guillaume de Flavy. His news for her was that the situation had worsened even in the short time she had been away. The enemy had occupied more villages, so that a hostile arc stretched along the north bank of the Oise facing the town, though its nearest point was more than two miles away, and Compiègne itself lay on the south bank. So the situation, though serious, was not yet desperate.

Now we come to the capture of Joan. Its circumstances were not grand. It was not an affair of a great battlefield with huge armies fighting to the death and a kingdom at stake. The action in which it happened was an unnecessary and pointless scuffle, more like a street-corner brawl than a battle.

Compiègne, as I have just said, lay on the south bank of the Oise. A bridge linked it with the north bank. The town end of this bridge was a drawbridge. Joan arrived in Compiègne at dawn. She heard Mass, slept, and then decided to make a sortie. De Flavy provided her with some men. Put with hers, they gave her a force of about five hundred. We have a description of her as she set out. It is the last time we shall see her free. "She mounted her horse, dressed and armed like a man. Over her armor was a coat of scarlet and gold. She rode a proud, magnificent charger, and her bearing was that of a captain leading a large host. And so, around four o'clock in the afternoon, with her standard high and fluttering in the wind, and with many nobles in her train, she left the town across the bridge." De Flavy took proper precautions. He ranged archers along the ramparts to cover the retreat of the party, stationed a few troops by the bridgehead, and placed boats on the river to ferry back any stragglers who might be in danger of being cut off. They were usual, routine steps, but it is certain that no serious danger was expected.

The French cavalcade rode across the meadows and up a hill, on the summit of which was the hamlet of Margny, a Burgundian outpost. Its garrison was unprepared for any attack and was soon in difficulties under the French onslaught. It seemed as though the French would massacre them, burn down the houses, and withdraw unscathed to Compiègne. But the moment of the attack was the moment when Jean de Luxembourg, one of the Duke of Burgundy's chief captains, and his staff chose to approach Margny on a tour of inspection of their outposts. He instantly sent messengers to three neighboring villages for reinforcements. One of these villages was north of Margny, and reinforcements from there meant little danger, as the French could make a fighting retreat in face of them. But another of the villages lay due west of Compiègne and the other due east. Troops advancing from them would meet at the bridge, and the French would have to cut their way through them as well as meet the attacking force from the north.

The Burgundians from the village to the north arrived, and it was not long before the French realized they were out-numbered—not heavily, though—and they began a slow retreat down the hill and to the bridge. Suddenly they caught sight of English troops moving along the riverbank from the west and other enemy troops coming in from the east. Panic seized most of them. In a moment a disciplined force making an orderly retreat became a fleeing rabble. Joan was swept into flight with them for a little way. Nearly all of them reached the bridge, but at the same time as the English. The bowmen on the walls were unable to fire for fear of killing their comrades. The French managed to fight their way onto the bridge, disengage for a few seconds, and rush into the safety of the town. De Flavy instantly ordered the drawbridge to be raised. Joan, with a tiny band of supporters, was left fighting in the meadow. "We're lost if we don't get back to the town," they shouted to her. She still thought victory could be theirs and cried, "Play your part and we shall beat them. Forward and they are ours!" They dragged at her horse's bridle and swung her around to face the town. It was in their mind to charge the English, smash through them, and then perhaps hold them at bay until the drawbridge could be lowered and Joan let in. But it was too late. The English were far too thick around the bridge. The enemy closed in on the little group. A bowman from Picardy named Lyonnel grasped Joan's coat and pulled her from her horse. He said he was of noble birth, and it was to him that she surrendered. The time was six o'clock, the day May 23, the year 1430.

De Flavy, the governor of Compiègne, was either a fool or a coward, possibly both. To raise his drawbridge and leave the stragglers stranded, particularly when Joan was one of them, was a piece of appalling misjudgment. The right, natural, and easy thing to do was to lead forth a body of troops the moment he saw Joan's party in difficulties. He could comfortably have routed the English and the Burgundians and ensured that Joan reached safety. Perhaps, though, it is unfair to judge him too harshly. Her voices had warned Joan that she was to be captured, so it may have been that de Flavy was but their instrument.

Anyhow, Joan was caught and at once, while she was still in the meadows opposite Compiègne, the Duke of Burgundy rode over to see her. What passed at this meeting is not recorded, but that evening the Duke had letters written and sent to all the chief towns of his territories: "The fame of this capture shall spread throughout the world and the news of it will expose the error and foolish beliefs of those who looked favorably upon the activities of this woman."

Throughout the part of France loyal to the King, news of Joan's capture brought grief and consternation. Public prayers for her deliverance were offered in every church. The Archbishop of Embrun, Jacques Gelu, a supporter of Joan and the author of a treatise about her which urged the King to follow her guidance, wrote at once to Charles, beseeching him to do everything possible to win her freedom. "To ransom and recover this girl, you must spare neither means nor money. If you do, you will be disgraced forever for monstrous ingratitude."

It is not known whether or not Charles was moved by this plea. If he was, he did singularly little about it. In this crisis he shows himself as a very mean, shabby, and contemptible figure. He never raised a finger to try to save Joan. He could have ransomed her, giving if need be a promise that he would never use her in the field again and, by the code of chivalry, such an offer of ransom would have had to be accepted. When Joan was placed in the power of the Bishop of Beauvais—which was French—the Archbishop of Rheims, his ecclesiastical superior, should have been ordered by the King to compel him to lodge her in the ecclesiastical prison in Beauvais, where, as the question of her orthodoxy was in dispute, she could be examined by theologians of both political parties. Such an order by the Archbishop would have been backed by the authority of Rome. But there is no record that Charles made any move to save the girl who saved his kingdom. He gave an example of callous ingratitude hard to match anywhere in history.

6. The Trial and the Fire

THE ARCHER who captured Joan was in the service of the Bastard of Wendomme, who served Jean de Luxembourg; Jean de Luxembourg was the vassal of the Duke of Burgundy, who in his turn was the vassal of the King of England. So by feudal law she was ultimately the prisoner of the King of England; but, also, by feudal law, each of the men named above, from the archer to the Duke, was entitled to some reward for passing her on to his superior. The archer was given a small sum, the Bastard considerably more, and Joan became the personal prisoner of Jean de Luxembourg, who of course could do nothing about her without the consent of the Duke of Burgundy.

The matter was complicated, too, by the fact that the ecclesiastics of England and Burgundy regarded Joan as a heretic in the service of the devil and so demanded that she should be immediately handed over to them. As she had been captured in the diocese of Beauvais, she came within the jurisdiction of its bishop, Pierre Cauchon. As Beauvais was in the hands of the French, he lived in Rouen. He was a former rector of the University of Paris, which at that time was the foremost in the Western world. "Foremost" is really a wholly inadequate word to describe its status and position. It was the largest in number of students and the standard of its learning was unsurpassed; but, far outweighing these points, were the weight and authority carried by its theological pronouncements. When the university gave a decision upon a matter of theology, it was heard throughout Christendom. It was called "a second Rome."

Only three days after her capture, the Vicar-General of the Inquisition in France wrote to the Duke of Burgundy and asked that Joan be given to the Inquisition so that she could be examined by the "good doctors and masters of the University of Paris." The Duke ignored the demand. The university then wrote to him again and also to Jean de Luxembourg. It seems that the university could not believe that Charles would make no effort to set Joan free. "We greatly fear that she may in some manner be taken from your power, that our enemies may try to set the woman free by paying a ransom." The university was also surprised that the Duke of Burgundy had not seen fit to answer the first approach made to him about Joan: "Notwithstanding, most feared and honored lord, our letter to your highness, imploring you humbly that the woman known as the Maid should be surrendered to the justice of the Church so that trial should be made of her idolatries and other matters concerning our holy faith, we have had no reply, nor have we learned that anything has been done toward handing over this woman . . . most feared and sovereign lord, we humbly beg you again that it may please you to transfer this woman into the hands of the Inquisitor of the Faith and to send her safely thither or have her surrendered to my lord bishop of Beauvais, in whose spiritual jurisdiction she was apprehended, that he may try her in matters of faith."

The Duke, however, though he was quite willing to allow the university to give its opinions on any point of theology it pleased and to listen to them with a tolerant respect, was very powerful in all temporal affairs. He knew his power and refused to be hustled by a collection of clerks and scholars, no matter how august. There was much hard bargaining before he released Joan from his grip. Pierre Cauchon went in person to the Burgundian camp, more letters were written, and it was not until November 21 that Joan was delivered to the English, and it cost them ten thousand gold crowns,—about two hundred and thirty thousand dollars—in ransom money.

During the early months of her captivity Joan was not treated harshly. After a day or two spent in Jean de Luxembourg's camp, she was taken to Noyon and from there to the castle of Beaulieu, about twenty miles north of Compiègne. She tried to escape, planning to lock her guards in the tower room which was her prison, but a chance meeting with the gatekeeper spoiled her plan. After two months at Beaulieu she was moved north again to Beaurevoir, near Cambrai, the castle of Jean de Luxembourg. There she was treated kindly by his wife and aunt, who both tried to persuade her to wear women's clothes. They offered her dresses or material from which to make her own. Joan refused, but at her trial said she was sorry not to be able to comply with their wishes as, apart from the Queen, there were no women in France whom she would rather have pleased. But God would not allow her to change the manner of her dress.

It was during her time at Beaurevoir that there occurred the strangest incident of her career. She jumped from the top of the castle tower, fell seventy feet to the ground, and was unhurt. The only ill effect she suffered was that she was unable to eat for two or three days. At her trial she was asked why she had jumped. She said, "I heard that the people of Compiègne were to be slaughtered when the town fell, and I felt that I would sooner die than go on living after so many good people had been killed. Another reason I jumped was because I knew I was going to be sold to the English, and I would rather have died than fall into their hands. St. Catherine told me not to jump, as

God would help the people of Compiègne and would help me too. I told her that if God was going to help the people of Compiègne I wanted to be there. She said, 'You must not weaken and must be resigned. You will not be freed until you have seen the King of England.' I told her, 'I do not want to see him and would rather die than fall into the hands of the English.' Afterward St. Catherine told me to ask God to forgive me for leaping off the tower and she promised that Compiègne would be relieved before Martinmas [November 11].'' Which it was.

There is no doubt that this incident happened. It is as well attested as any event in history and owes nothing to the imagination of pious hagiographers. There are three extraordinary things about it. She was unhurt after falling from a height of seventy feet, a fact for which there can be no natural explanation. It is always presumed that she made the leap to escape. This view is based on her saying that she wanted to go to Compiègne, but it ignores the fact that she also said she would sooner die than fall into the hands of the English and that she admitted that one of the reasons for her jumping was that she knew she was going to be handed over to them. Something very near to suicide was in Joan's mind. I think her attitude was: I may escape and, anyhow, if I don't I shall kill myself and so escape the English. The third astonishing aspect of the incident is that Joan defied St. Catherine's warning to her not to jump. We have seen what full and instant obedience Joan always gave to the orders of her voices, yet here she disobeys one of her heavenly guides to perform an act which, if it had brought its natural consequence, would have been a mortal sin. That she was unhurt and did not die was a miracle; that she jumped shows that she was an unhappy, desperate, and forsaken girl, and we should be grateful for yet another example of a saint who sinned because, like us all, she was a human being.

A knight by the name of Aimond de Macy, who was at Beaurevoir, reports that he spoke to her quite often and says that several times he attempted to make unchaste advances toward her but that Joan pushed him away with all her strength. He states: "She was a most modest girl, both in her speech and in her behavior."

Finally, as she had feared, she was sold to the English, and from Beaurevoir she was taken to Arras, then on to the castle of Drugy, then to the castle of Crotoy on the mouth of the Somme. Everywhere she was treated as a prisoner of consequence and people flocked from the neighboring towns to see her. They were kind, so kind that Joan was impelled to exclaim, "What nice people they are! I should be very happy— when I come to die—if I could be buried among them." At Crotoy one of the other prisoners was a priest, and Joan confessed to him and received Holy Communion. She went by boat across the mouth of the Somme to St. Valéry, the little village where, five hundred and ten years later, a handful of the Godons whose ancestors she feared and some of her own French stood with their backs to the sea and together tried to hold off the German barbarians. The rest of her journey was soon over—to Eu, to Dippe, and on to Rouen. There she was placed in one of the towers of the town's castle. The time was December; she had five months of life left to her.

Who was responsible for her death? Some Frenchmen, their intelligence muddied by a warm and excessive patriotism, put all the blame on the English. To read and believe their outpourings would leave one with a picture of virtuous French clerics fighting tooth and nail to save Joan from the stake but being overborne by the malignant power, remorselessly applied, of the English lords. As an Englishman, I feel for my country what a good Frenchman feels for his, but—and I confess it gladly—my love of England is almost matched by my fondness for France. So I can perhaps be impartial in assessing the degree of guilt borne by the English and the French.

There is not a shadow of doubt that the English meant to kill Joan and were determined to stick at nothing to have her dead. We have the letter from Henry VI of England—in reality, of course, from the Council of Regency—to the Bishop of Beauvais, in which the English are ordered to deliver Joan to him, "so that he may examine and question her and proceed against her according to God, the divine law, and the holy canons." The letter lists various crimes of which it claims Joan is guilty and ends with the sinister sentence: "Nevertheless, we intend to seize and regain possession of this Joan if it should happen that she is not convicted or found guilty of the said crimes."

Why then, we may well ask, go through the farce of a trial which, whatever the verdict, would still have a fatal outcome for Joan? For the English were wholly without conscience or mercy. A few months after Joan's death in the market square of Rouen, a hundred and four Frenchmen were executed in the same square. They were prisoners of war and their only crime was that they had fought for their country. Joan could have been publicly executed without any trial or quietly murdered in her cell. The English certainly wanted her dead, but they also wanted her discredited. She had to be declared a heretic and inspired by demons. A condemnation on such grounds would condemn Charles equally. He would stand before the world as a pretender to the French throne whose invalid coronation was only made possible by a witch. The recent French victories could also be dismissed as the work of witchcraft. So it was, in the English view, essential that Joan be condemned by an ecclesiastical court with the authority of the University of Paris behind it. State trials are very much the same in any century.

Some of the French who conducted the trial showed great zeal for the job. This is not only my opinion. It is that of men involved in the trial and who later gave evidence during the rehabilitation process. They said, "Some acted out of fear and some out of zeal for the English party. I do not believe that the judges were under great pressure. I believe that it was more a matter of bribery, as some of them certainly accepted presents." Another opinion: "Some of the court were forced to act against their will and showed great fear, but another section took part quite voluntarily and sided with the English." A third view: "The English instituted the prosecution and they paid for it. I do not think, however, that the Bishop of Beauvais was compelled to prosecute Joan, nor was the promoter of the case, Jean d'Estivet. They did what they did of their own free will."

When all the arguments as to responsibility have been heard, there remains one certain fact: French priests and lawyers tried and condemned Joan, and every witness against her was French. None of them need have taken part in the trial. They could have left the dirty work to an English ecclesiastical court. As it was, five bishops, thirty-two doctors of theology, sixteen bachelors of theology, nine doctors of civil and canon law, seven doctors of medicine, and more than eighty other priests and lawyers were involved in her trial. Except five, every one of them was French. Only a handful of them were obviously well disposed toward Joan, at least in the earlier stages of her trial.

She was, as I have said, imprisoned in one of the towers of

the castle of Rouen. She was not being tried for any political offense. She was accused of heresy. It was an ecclesiastical court which dealt with her, and so she should have been kept in an ecclesiastical prison where her jailers would have been women.

Her room was large, about forty-three paces across. It was gloomy, as some of the window slits had been bricked in. Her ankles were fettered so that she could take only short steps. Around her waist was a chain fastened to a great baulk of timber five feet long. A story exists that she was kept in an iron cage in this room. Three men who were in Rouen at the time speak of this cage. One says, "I heard from Etienne Castille, the blacksmith, that he made an iron cage for her in which she was fastened by the neck, the hands, and the feet and that she was kept in it from the time she was brought to Rouen until her trial began," but he adds, "I never saw her in it." Another says, "I saw the cage being weighed," but he too adds, "I did not see Joan in the cage." Joan complained about the conditions in which she was imprisoned, but she never mentions this cage. Five English soldiers "of the lowest sort" guarded her. Three stayed in the room at night, the other two were stationed outside the door. "They were most eager for her death and often mocked her." The also tried to rape her. The Earl of Warwick heard of this, severely warned them against molesting her, and replaced two of them. But they remained a brutal and unsavory crew and the cause of much suffering for Joan. A Frenchman writing today has so far lost his calm and sense of style as to call them "pigs with human faces."

One of the assessors at the trial, Jean Fabri, an Augustinian monk and later a bishop, gave evidence years later: "I do not know how it came about that she was imprisoned in the castle at Rouen. It greatly displeased some of us, however, that she was not put in an ecclesiastical prison. I complained about it myself. Since she had been handed over to the Church, it seemed quite wrong to put her in the hands of laymen and particularly of Englishmen."

A more unpleasant character altogether than the soldiers, though, was a canon of Rouen Cathedral, one Nicolas Loiseleur. Before her trial he visited her several times, pretending to be a native of Lorraine and a prisoner of the English. He offered to hear her confession. He managed to gain her confidence and gave a report of all she told him to Cauchon. A hole was bored in the wall of Joan's room and her talks with Loiseleur were overheard by a little group of notaries. He often urged her to put no trust in the Churchmen, "for if you believe them, they will trick you and you will certainly die."

Before her trial she was also visited, on the orders of the Duchess of Bedford, by a group of matrons who examined her to see if she was a virgin. She was.

Cauchon was determined, so he said, to hold a "model trial." By this he meant a trial which would be legally unassailable, and he devoted as much care to the task as any prosecutor in the various state trials which have disgraced this century. He failed, mainly because he could not have imagined that the proceedings he controlled and initiated would, in just under twenty-five years later, be so closely and thoroughly examined. Had he foreseen that every detail of the trial would be probed into and that many officers of his court would give evidence on oath about its activities, he no doubt would have taken even greater care to try to make it appear that he conducted a just trial.

Ecclesiastical trials in fifteenth-century France always had two stages. First of all was the "preparatory process." In this, the men responsible for launching the trial gathered together what evidence they could about the prisoner and his alleged crime. On the basis of this evidence they formulated a precise charge against him, and it was on this same evidence that the prosecutor based his case. But the court, if it considered the evidence warranted, could dismiss the accused person. Two judges did this work, together with any number of assessors they chose to appoint. Each one of them could question witnesses and the accused and contribute in any way he thought fit to arriving at a proper decision. The two judges alone had the final word. When this preparatory process was over, the prosecutor assembled all the material it had produced and from it prepared his indictment, which was then put before the court, whose members were the same as those who held the preparatory process. The prisoner was examined on every article in the indictment and his replies written down after each of them. This examination of the prisoner was known as the "ordinary process." It was, in fact, the trial proper. On the resulting document—the indictment and the prisoner's replies—the court based its verdict. If it found the prisoner guilty, it admonished him and pronounced sentence. The moment he was found guilty, the prisoner might repent and abjure his errors. If he did, he would escape death and, according to the gravity of his offense, would be sentenced to a long or short term of imprisonment or some act of penance not necessarily involving imprisonment. If, however, he showed no sign of repentance, the court handed him over to secular justice and asked the officers of that justice to show him mercy. Within five days of the handing over of the condemned person, he had to be burned at the stake. If the lay law officers obeyed the words if the ecclesiastical court and showed mercy, they would promptly have been charged with condoning heresy and would themselves be led to the stake. The Church refused to execute a heretic, but it insisted that the State should do the work. As a medieval judge said, "What one begins, the other finishes."

A trial of a heretic could also be taken up again even after sentence had been passed. If the guilty person recanted he could, as we have seen, be spared death. But if, after his forgiveness and reception back into the Church, he lapsed into heresy again, he would at once be given a most speedy trial in which the only point at issue would be whether or not he had lapsed. In nine cases out of ten a mere suspicion of lapse was fatal and condemnation on such a charge meant certain death. No second recantation was ever allowed.

Before Joan's trial, Couchon had sent investigators to Domrémy and the surrounding district to collect accounts of Joan's life there, and he had examined the findings of the ecclesiastical court of Poitiers which investigated Joan's integrity soon after she first appeared before the King at Chinon. No facts injurious to her had come to light, but we shall see how the worst interpretation was put upon some of them and how they were twisted so they became fatal for Joan.

It was on February 21, 1431, that Joan made her first appearance before the men who were to martyr her. She was served with a formal summons to appear. She replied that she was willing, but she made two demands: that the court should consist of an equal number of clerics who supported the French and of those who supported the English, and also asked to be allowed to attend Mass. Neither demand was granted. She was led into the chapel of the castle with her feet shackled and allowed to sit on a stool. Confronting her was the Bishop of

Beauvais, Cauchon; the Vicar in Rouen of the Inquisitor of France, Jean Lemaistre; the prosecutor, Jean d'Estivet; and forty assessors. There were a handful of decent men among them, men who were kind, fair, and honest. The rest were a sorry bunch. Some had sold themselves completely to the English and were willing to swear black was white at a word from their masters; others were desiccated theological lawyers versed in all the logic of the schools but empty of any drop of charity; a few were so horrified by the words "witch" and "heretic" that all reason and calm judgment left them. The greatest scoundrel of them all was the prosecutor, Jean d'Estivet, a brutal, foul-mouthed man who openly, though vainly, tried to browbeat and terrorize Joan. One of his officers, Jean Massieu, tells this story of him: "When I used to lead Joan from her cell to the courtroom, I passed the chapel and, at her request, used to stop there and let her say her prayers. But Jean d'Estivet caught me doing it one day and burst out: 'What do you mean by letting that excommunicated whore come near here without permission? Do it once again and I'll see you're put in a place where you won't see the sun or the moon for a month.' But I disobeyed him, so he used to stand in front of the chapel door and prevent her entrance."

At eight o'clock on that February morning—it was a Wednesday—Joan saw these clerics ranged in a double half circle before her. They saw a young girl in male clothing with a bare head and short clipped hair. It can be very safely assumed that they had never seen such a figure of a woman. All of them were startled and most shocked. We must be fair to them about this. They felt exactly the same kind of shock as a last-century court would have felt if a young woman defendant had stepped into the dock stark-naked. In an age when jeans and leotards have become the uniform of the teen-age girl, this sense of outrage may astonish us, but we must accept that it did exist and was quite genuine.

The first thing Joan was asked to do was to take an oath to tell the truth.

She replied, "I don't know what you want to question me about. You may ask me things I won't tell you."

Cauchon asked, "Will you swear to speak the truth about matters of faith?"

"I'll willingly take the oath about what concerns my life at home and about what I have done since I rode into France," Joan said, "but I have only spoken about God's revelations to me to the King and I will say nothing of them here even if it means having my head cut off. I have no right to tell you what I hear from my voices, but in a week's time I may know if I am allowed to reveal them."

Cauchon repeatedly exhorted her to take the oath on his terms and she repeatedly refused. Finally Joan knelt, placed both her hands on the Missal offered her, and swore to answer truthfully every question about anything except the revelations made to her. And with that Cauchon had to be content.

She was asked about her childhood and, when she said her mother had taught her to say the Our Father, the Hail Mary, and the Credo, she had another brush with Cauchon. He told her to say the Our Father.

"Certainly," Joan declared, "I'll gladly say it for you if you'll hear my confession." Cauchon repeated his order again and again, and Joan refused again and again to obey. Cauchon told her he would send a couple of notable priests to her in private to hear her say the Our Father. Joan said, "Send them, but I shall not say it to them except in confession."

Cauchon had to leave this point. He went on to forbid her to try to escape from her prison, saying that if she did escape she would be automatically convicted of heresy, as she would be flouting the authority of the Church.

"I do not accept that," she told him. "I have never taken an oath not to escape. I have wanted and still want to escape, and that is a lawful desire for any prisoner."

With this reply flung at him, Cauchon at once summoned three English men-at-arms and made them take an oath to guard her closely. Henceforth these three men were in charge of the ordinary soldiers who guarded her.

That was all that was accomplished at this first session of the court at which Joan was present.

Next day the court met in the robing room at the end of the great hall of the castle, and the session opened with another argument about Joan's oath. She told them, "I swore yesterday and that should be quite enough." And again she swore a conditional oath.

One of the assessors rose to question her, but before he began she said to him, "If you really knew the truth about me, you would not want me in your power. I have done nothing except what I was told to do by God." This session was spent in questioning her about her life in Domrémy, her visits to Vaucouleurs, and her journey to Chinon.

We must not imagine that during any of the examinations there was an orderly procession of question and answer or that the atmosphere was that of a quiet courtroom. Every effort was made to confuse and browbeat Joan. This is what some of those who took part in the trial had to say about it: "Before she had answered one member of the court, another would fling a further question at her, and so she was often hurried and confused in her replies. She often said to her interrogators, 'My lords, please take your turn' . . . they often asked Joan questions in several parts and some of them asked her difficult questions at the same time. Then, before she had time to reply to one, another asked her a fresh question. I was amazed at seeing how well she was able to reply to the very subtle and tricky questions that were asked her, for a scholar would have been hard pressed to answer well. The examination usually went on for from eight to eleven hours . . . I once saw one of the abbots questioning Joan and then another assessor intervened with several different questions. So she told them they were greatly prejudicing her by harassing her with such a stream of questions . . . they kept switching from subject to subject . . . sometimes they questioned her without a moment's pause for two to three hours."

At the next session there was another attempt to make her swear a comprehensive oath, and again she refused. She warned her judges, "Take great care of what you say, for, as my judges, you are assuming a terrible responsibility." Speaking directly to Cauchon, she said, "You declare that you are my judge. Very well, but take good heed of what you do, because I am truly sent from God and you are putting yourself in great peril." Much of this day was devoted to the question of her voices. One of the theologians, trying to show they were hallucinations produced by her physical condition, asked her when she had last had food and drink. Not since noon of the preceding day, she told him. "And when did you last hear your voices?" "Three times yesterday and once today. I was wakened by a voice yesterday morning. I don't know if it was actually in the room, but it was in the castle. I sat up in bed, put my hands together, and thanked it and asked it for counsel. It told me to answer boldly and it told me the same last night. And this voice comes from God—and I believe that as firmly as I believe in the Catholic faith and that Our Lord redeemed us from the pains of hell."

It was then that she was asked, "Are you in a state of grace?" If she answered yes, she would show highly dangerous presumption; if she answered no, she would be making an equally dangerous confession of sin. One of the assessors protested against her being asked such a question, and to him the Bishop of Beauvais turned and snapped, "It would be better if you kept your mouth shut!" But Joan took this loaded question— "Are you in a state of grace?"—in her stride: "If I am not, may God put me there; if I am, may God keep me there. I would sooner die than not be in the love of God." One of the clerks records: "Her interrogators were astonished at her answer and they asked her nothing else for some time." She was young and without a trace of education, yet the sense and aptness of her replies amazed many of those in court. "She answered the questions with as much wisdom as the most learned scholar could have done . . . if some of the theologians there had had to answer such questions, they would not have replied as sensibly . . . her answers were so very wise that I thought she was inspired . . . in her bearing she was very simple, but her answers were packed with wisdom and discernment."

After the question about grace, she was asked more about Domrémy, and every effort was made to prove that she had been involved in magical practices centering around the Ladies' Tree, the great beech on which the young girls of the village used to hang garlands. The matter of clothing was again brought up, and she was asked if she wanted a woman's dress. "Give me one," she said, "and I will put it on and go away from here. Otherwise I will not wear it, but will be satisfied with what I have on, for it pleases God that I should be dressed as I am."

After this session Joan fell ill and there was a break of three days in the proceedings. A doctor was sent to her. "I felt her pulse and asked her what was wrong and if she was in pain. She told me the Bishop of Beauvais had sent her a carp and she thought eating it had made her ill. Jean d'Estivet, who was present, called her a liar and a whore. 'It's you, you whore, who've been eating herrings and other things which have made you ill.' She denied this, and they began to abuse each other." It has been foolishly suggested that Cauchon did, in fact, send her a poisoned fish. I can think of nothing more unlikely. The very last thing he or the English wanted was for her to die a natural death. On this we have the evidence of another doctor who was summoned to her cell by the Cardinal of England and the Earl of Warwick: "The Earl told us that the King of England would not at any cost have her die except at the hands of the law. He wanted to have her burned. When we decided to bleed her, the Earl said: 'Be very careful! She's so cunning she might kill herself.' But she was bled and quickly picked up." So Cauchon must have been a very worried man when she fell ill. That weekend was not, in any way, a pleasant one for him.

Besides Joan's illness, another disturbing incident occurred. Cauchon was anxious, as we have seen, to make the trial a very correct and well-run one. A highly respected authority on canon law, a Norman priest called Jean Lohier, arrived in Rouen as Joan fell ill. Cauchon assembled all the documents concerning the trial, took them round to Lohier's lodgings, and asked him for his opinion of the case. Lohier studied the papers and promptly declared that the trial was invalid. He gave as his reasons: "The trial is not following the regular and proper procedure of such trials. It is being conducted in what is virtually a private court, and those taking part are not fully and completely free to give their honest opinion. The honor of the King of France is involved, as she champions his cause, yet he has not been asked to appear, nor is he represented by anyone. In addition, no written charges have been produced and this simple girl has no counsel and is left on her own to answer questions on very serious matters put to her by the most learned theologians." This verdict by Lohier shook Cauchon profoundly. He at once hurried away to consult a small, intimate circle of his confederates. He told them, "If we are to believe Lohier, we ought to start the trial all over again, for what we've done so far is useless." There was a long and serious discussion, but at the end Cauchon decided to stand firm. "By St. John, we won't stop. We'll carry on with the trial as we've started it."

Next morning one of the two notaries at the trial met Lohier outside the church of Notre-Dame and asked him what he thought of the trial. Lohier declared, "They will catch her out, if they can manage it, with her own words, especially with what she says about her visions and voices. If only she would not say, 'I'm sure about them.' There's no one on earth could find her guilty if she would only say, 'It seems to me,' instead of 'I am sure.' Most of the people at the trial seem to be spurred on by hatred and so I am not going to stay, for I mean to take no further part in the business."

He was as good as his word. He left Rouen at once and had nothing more to do with the trial.

At the interrogation which followed her illness, Joan several times urged her judges to send to Poitiers for the record of her examination there. Needless to say, her urgings were ignored, but it seems as if Joan was beginning to realize a fundamental weakness in the very basis of the court before which she stood. At Poitiers equally learned clerics had been assembled, called together by the Archbishop of Rheims, the immediate spiritual superior of the Bishop of Beauvais. As a court, its authority was higher than that at Rouen. It had found her innocent of all heresy, and yet the Rouen court was putting a completely different interpretation on sayings and events which Poitiers had considered earlier and found quite without harm.

It would here, I think, be well to transcribe a fair sample of the kind of questioning to which she was subjected, together with her answers. It is more than five hundred years ago. The courtroom is cold; the sounds and smells are all different; no noise of automobiles from the street outside, no smell of gasoline or stale tobacco smoke; the daylight is clearer than ours and human voices are louder and, even in a town, the sounds of the countryside are everywhere. Joan is very pale. Her bout of illness has increased her prison pallor. She is not nervous, though perhaps a little irritable from time to time, but neither cowed by nor afraid of the men she believes are hounding her to the stake.

And now the questions:

"Did God order you to wear a man's clothes?"

"My clothes are a trifle. They are of no importance."

"Did any man suggest you wear them?"

"No. I put them on, I have done everything, at the command of God and the angels."

"Do you think that command is lawful?"

"I repeat: all I have done is at God's command, and if He

had ordered me to wear different clothes, I should have done so, for I obey His commands. And all I have done at His command is well done."

"When you hear your voices, do you see a light?"

"There is always a lot of light, which I think is very fitting."

"What do your voices sound like?"

"They are soft and low."

"Does St. Margaret speak in English?"

"Why should she? She's not on the side of the English."

"Has St. Michael any hair?"

"Who would cut it off?"

"Is he naked?"

"Do you think God can't afford to clothe him?"

(As Sainte-Beuve says: "The thing about these clerics which particularly strikes one is their stupidity and materialism. They grasp absolutely nothing of Joan's inspiration and their questions never cease trying—but without success—to debase and coarsen her.")

"Do you believe you are in a state of mortal sin?"

"Please God I never was in such a state and, if it please Him, I never shall do anything to burden my soul so greatly."

"You have said we are putting ourselves in great danger by trying you. What do you mean? What kind of danger?"

"You, the bishop, say you're my judge. I don't know if you are, but be very careful to judge me fairly. Otherwise, you will be in great peril. I'm giving you this warning so that if God punishes you I shall have done my duty."

"But what is the danger?"

She did not answer this, but said, "St. Catherine has told me. I shall be given help. All my voices say: 'Take everything calmly. Do not be concerned about your martyrdom. In the end, you will come to Paradise.' "

"Well, then, are you sure of your salvation and sure that you will not be damned in hell?"

"I believe what my voices say."

"Do you believe you cannot commit mortal sin?"

"I don't know. In all things I commit myself to God."

"Do you think you are in mortal sin now?"

"I don't think so. Anyhow, it is a matter for God and for a priest in confession."

"Which would you prefer? To hear Mass dressed as a woman, or to stay dressed as you are and not hear Mass?"

"I'll tell you if you promise me that I may hear Mass if I wear a woman's dress."

"Very well. I promise that you may hear Mass if you are in a woman's dress."

"And what do you say if I have sworn and promised our Lord not to put off my present clothes? But anyhow, have a long dress made for me which reaches down to the ground but with a train, and give it me to go to Mass. When I have heard Mass and come back, I will put on my men's clothes again."

"Why won't you take a woman's dress without any conditions?"

"Give me a long dress such as the daughters of your citizens wear and I will wear it to go and hear Mass."

After March 3, Joan was questioned by a smaller group of men. This series of questioning lasted till March 17 and took place in her cell. Again she had to reply to a multitude of questions. They ranged over the same ground—questions about her dress, her voices, her leap from the walls of Beaurevoir, whether she had taken part in magical ceremonies around the

Ladies' Tree in Domrémy, whether she had put a spell on her pennant. Then something new was put to her. It was the exceedingly dangerous question: "Will you submit what you have said and done to the decision of the Church?"

Her reply was, "All I have said and done is in the hand of God and I commit myself to Him. I would neither say nor do anything against the Christian faith, and if I held anything which the clergy should declare to be against that faith, I would not hold fast to it, but would cast it from me."

Now this was not a satisfactory answer in any way. The "clergy" are not the Church, nor does Joan say what members of the clergy she would obey. She could have had in mind those ecclesiastics of Poitiers who had long ago found her without fault.

She was asked again if she would submit to the decision of the Church.

This time she answered, "I commit myself to Our Lord, Who sent me, to our Lady, and to all the blessed saints of Paradise. Our Lord and the Church are all one, so why do you make difficulties?"

The report of the trial continues: "She was told that there is the Church Triumphant, where God is together with the saints and all the souls who are already saved; there is also the Church Militant, and that consists of our Holy Father the Pope, the Vicar of Christ on earth, the prelates of the Church, the clergy, and all good Catholics. This Church in good assembly cannot err under the guidance of the Holy Ghost. Therefore, she was asked if she would submit to the Church Militant; that is, the Church on earth. She answered that she came to the king of France in God's name and in the name of the Blessed Virgin and of all the blessed saints in Paradise and of the Church Triumphant above. It was to that Church that she submitted all her good deeds and all she had done or should do. And she would do nothing more about her submission to the Church Militant." The report says that in the afternoon session of that same day she was "asked whether she did not think she was bound to tell the whole truth to the Pope concerning all that she should be asked on matters of faith and conscience. She answered that she demanded to be led before him, and then she would answer all that was required."

So at this stage in her trial Joan refuses to submit to the Church, as she understands it, but asks to be taken to the Pope. Her examiners will return to this matter, and so shall we, when her trial is resumed.

There was now a short break, for the "preparatory process" had ended, and the indictment had to be drawn up for the trial proper. This trial began on Tuesday of Holy Week, March 27. The indictment consisted of seventy articles. They cover eighty-three pages of fairly close print. When Joan was led before the court, she was told by Cauchon that all her judges were learned men, well founded in canon law and in civil law, and that they intended to deal with her in piety and kindliness, not seeking vengeance or corporal punishment, but only her instruction and her return to the path of truth which led to salvation. Since they all knew she was not learned in such difficult matters, she should choose one or several of those present or, if she did not want to choose, he, the Bishop of Beauvais, would pick some one who would counsel her on what she should say, provided that she was ready to answer truthfully.

Joan answered, "I thank you and all here for considering my salvation, and I thank you for offering me counsel, but I have no intention of departing from the counsel of our Lord." By this time, it is clear, she had lost whatever belief she may once have had in the good faith of her judges. An incident next day may help to explain her attitude. The indictment was written in Latin, but it was translated and read in French to Joan on the Wednesday, Thursday, and Friday. Each article contained an accusation against her and ended with the reply she gave to it during the preparatory process. The first article, however, stated that the court was fully competent to judge the case, and Joan at once said that she knew that the Pope, bishops, and other clergy protected the Catholic faith and punished those who fell away from it, but that she submitted to the Church in heaven. She believed most firmly that she had remained true to the Catholic faith. At this, a Dominican priest, Friar Isambart de la Pierre, one of the assessors, leaned over to her and whispered the very sound advice that she should offer to submit to the General Council, for on it were many prelates and doctors who supported the King of France. This Council was that of Basle, which was then sitting. Joan at once told the court that she wanted to be taken before the Council.

Cauchon, the man who had offered to provide a priest to advise her, shouted at Isambart, "Keep quiet, in the devil's name!" The clerk recording the proceedings asked if he should record Joan's wish to go before the Council. The bishop told him it was not necessary. Joan turned to him and said, "Why do you have written down everything that is against me, but never anything that is for me?"

It was not the first time Isambart had been in trouble. During an earlier session of the trial, he and another Dominican, Guillaume Duval, sat near Joan. Duval says: "When she was being questioned, Isambart advised her what to say by touching her or giving her a sign. After the session I went with Isambart and one of the lawyers, Jean de la Fontaine, to visit Joan in her cell. The Earl of Warwick was there and he at once launched a violent attack against Isambart. He shouted at him, 'Why did you keep touching this wicked woman this morning? Why did you keep making signs to her? Let me catch you once again trying to help her and I'll have you flung in the Seine.'" Warwick then ordered that they should never again be allowed to visit Joan.

The charges made against Joan in the seventy articles were many and varied.

First it was stated that she had "called up demons and evil spirits, consulted and frequented them, and entered into pacts and treaties with them."

Then the third article rolls out this accusation wrapped in the pompous—but, in this case, deadly—jargon of lawyers: "The said accused has fallen into many and divers and most evil errors, all infected with heresy. She has said, declared, voiced, uttered, and impressed on the hearts of simple people certain false and lying propositions both tinged with heresy and actually heretical. They are contrary to our Catholic faith, against the statutes delivered and approved by the General Councils; they are scandalous and sacrilegious, contrary to good customs, and offensive to pious ears; she had given counsel, aid, and favor to those who have said, uttered, affirmed, and promulgated these propositions."

Four of the articles—and they are long ones—were concerned with her dress. They open with a great salvo of horrified prudery: "The said Joan attributes to God, His angels, and His saints instructions that are contrary to the virtue of women, forbidden by divine law, abominable to God and man, and forbidden under penalty of anathema by ecclesiastical law, such as the wearing of short and dissolute male clothes. She often dressed in rich and sumptuous clothing, in furs, in precious stuffs and cloth of gold, and not only did she wear short tunics, but also tabards and garments open at the sides. It is notorious that when she was captured she wore a loose cloak of golden cloth, a cap on her head, and her hair cut short like a man's. And, in general, having thrown aside all womanly modesty, not only to the scorn of all decent women, but also of all well-instructed men, she has worn the garments that the most dissolute of men are wont to wear and, in addition, she has carried weapons. To attribute these activities to the command of God, His holy angels and virgin saints, is to blaspheme our Lord, ignore the divine decrees, violate canon law, scandalize all womanly modesty, pervert all decency of outward bearing, and to give approval and encouragement to the worst kind of human behavior."

Her accusers return to this nearly forty articles further on: "The said Joan, heedless of her salvation and at the prompting of the devil, is not and has not been ashamed from time to time and in many different places to receive the Body of Christ when she was dressed in dissolute male attire, a costume forbidden her by the command of God and the Church."

Another charge sprang from false masculine pride: "The said Joan, against the bidding of God and His saints, proudly and presumptuously assumed domination over men. She made herself leader and captain of an army which at times had sixteen thousand men and in which there were princes and other nobles, and she made them all fight under her."

And there was, of course, a sense of outrage at her easy companionship with men: "She walked with men without shame and did not wish to have the company of women, preferring to employ only men whom she made serve in the private offices of her room and in her secret affairs, which is something unheard of in a devout and modest woman."

As we would expect, the matter of the voices received great attention: "The said Joan declared that she believed and still does believe that the spirits which appeared to her were angels, archangels, and saints as firmly as she believes in the Christian faith, although she reports no sign by which they can be recognized and she has consulted no bishop or any other priest to learn whether she should believe such spirits . . . she has venerated these spirits, kissing the earth where she saw them standing, kneeling in front of them, embracing and kissing them, yet she did not know if they were good spirits and indeed, considering the circumstances, they are plainly more evil than good. Her veneration of them seems to partake of idolatry and to come from a pact made with devils . . . she frequently and daily invokes these spirits, consulting them in her private actions, for example in the kind of answers she should make in her trial, which appear to be and is an invocation of demons."

In many of the articles she is accused of trafficking with demons. They claim that she put a spell on her standard, her sword, and a ring she wore; that she was accustomed when a very young girl to dance alone at night around the Ladies' Tree at Domrémy, chanting invocations and practicing evil arts; and that she carried a mandrake in her bosom, "hoping thereby to have good fortune, riches, and all the things of this world."

But the key article of these indictments is that concerned with her attitude toward the Church: "When she was asked whether she would submit to the decision of the Church on earth all that she had done, especially the crimes imputed to her and everything that concerns her case, she declared that she would submit to the Church Militant, always provided that we did not ask her to do what was impossible. By impossible, she meant denying those of her words and deeds which concern the visions and revelations she claims to have had from God. She would not deny them for anything in the world. Not for any man alive will she cease to do what Our Lord has bidden her. If the Church wished her to do anything against His bidding, nothing would make her obey. She was asked if she would submit to the Church, if the Church Militant said her revelations were false and the work of the devil, superstitious and evil. She said she would submit to Our Lord, for she will always do His will. All that she had done had been done at His bidding, and it would have been impossible for her to do otherwise. If the Church Militant told her to do differently, she would submit only to Our Lord. We asked her if she believes she is subject to the Church on earth—that is, to our Holy Father the Pope, to the cardinals and archbishops, bishops and other prelates of the Church. She said she did believe that, Our Lord being first served, her voices do not forbid her to obey the Church."

The presentation of these articles to Joan took place on Tuesday and Wednesday, March 27 and 28. On the following Saturday she was visited in her cell by Cauchon and several of his theologians. They again took up this crucial point of her willingness to submit to the Church. Her line was exactly the same, a willingness to submit with reservations.

Such a qualified yielding would have been fatal to her, even if she had been found innocent of all the other charges. Today, too, no Catholic could remain a Catholic if he took Joan's attitude, as she disclosed it at Rouen, to the Church Militant. For she was saying that her private revelations had more authority for her than the teaching voice of the Church, and that is the gravest of all heresies. It is one which, if pressed to its logical conclusion, denies that the Church has its authority from Our Lord and so denies that its authority in matters of faith is absolute. It is the Protestant heresy of exalting personal and private judgment above the judgment of the Church. So, on her showing at Rouen, Joan was a heretic and, by the standards of her day, deserved her fate.

Actually, it is not so simple as that. At Rouen, Joan saw Cauchon and his assistants as the Church Militant. She was, it is true, told what it really was, but it was not easy for so young, so uneducated, and so ill-used a girl to think of the Pope and the Councils of the Church when Cauchon stood before her and the stake was so very near. It is not surprising that she was unwilling to abandon herself unreservedly to the Rouen representatives of the Church Militant. She was very well aware that she had been found guiltless of heresy by equally learned clerics at Poitiers and, from her frequent references to that examination, it is clear she set great store by its verdict. At Poitiers the local representatives of the Church had given her and her mission their blessing; at Rouen, other local representatives of the same Church appeared to be hounding her to death. The Poitiers clerics said her voices came from God; those of Rouen told her they came from the devil. So we can see that she had some excuse for refusing to pledge instant and complete obedience to the Church Militant, as she saw it. That does not make her a heretic. She did ask repeatedly to be taken before the Pope and I cannot imagine that, had she been led before him, she would have persisted in the attitude she adopted at Rouen. She felt the men of Rouen were her enemies and the agents of the enemies of her country; she felt from the start that they were bent on her death and that, to kill her in a seemly, judicial manner, her voices must be wholly discredited; so, too, must she be, in the hope that her condemnation and death would hurt the cause of the King.

In such circumstances, it was very natural for her to insist on the reality of her voices and the truth of their message. She must have known instinctively that she was making her stand before a very small section of the Church and that it was a section moved more by political ambition than theological truth. We must always remember that Cauchon and the English ignored her plea to be taken before the Pope. This was not because her case was not considered of enough importance. Far from it. The moment she was safely dead, the University of Paris wrote to the Pope and to the College of Cardinals announcing the news, "so that it should not be said that silence has concealed what was done for the exaltation of the faith . . . this woman was superstitious, a prophetess, a trafficker with demons, idolatrous, a blasphemer of God and the saints, and in every way erring in the faith of Jesus Christ." In its letter to the Pope, the university lied: "When this woman learned that she was soon to die, she confessed before many people and with great lamentations that she had been mocked and deceived by the spirits which she said had appeared to her." There is not a word of truth in that. Letters were also sent, as from the King of England, to the rulers of every European state, similar to those from the university and telling the same lie.

A king and a university of the standing of Paris do not see fit to write to the Pope and fellow monarchs about the routine trial and execution of an unimportant girl. The English and Cauchon realized very well what they were about and knew that it was right and desirable, by canon law, that Joan's appeal to the Pope should have been heard and acted upon. They no doubt also realized that the Pope would find no wrong in her.

After the seventy articles had been read to Joan, it was decided to boil them down to twelve articles and to send them to "doctors and other men learned in canon and civil law, requesting their advice for the good of the Faith." At first sight this seems a not unfair thing to do, but once we examine the twelve articles, it is plain that their production is just another move to get Joan condemned. The articles are short, and many allegations against Joan have been skillfully condensed and her denials and explanations omitted. Nowhere in them, for example, is there any mention that Joan had appealed to the Pope.

Copies of these twelve articles were put in the hands of all the clerics concerned with the case who were in Rouen. This was done on April 5. A week later, sixteen doctors and six bachelors of theology gave their collective verdict: Joan was blasphemous and a heretic. Individual replies then began to arrive. They were not all of the kind to satisfy Cauchon. Three bachelors of theology had the courage to declare that they could find nothing necessarily diabolic in the origin of her revelations. Another bachelor of theology (and let us record his name—Raoul le Sauvage) shows a rare humanity: "It is proper, my reverend father and my lords, to take into account the frailty of womankind, and she should be charitably admonished to reform, and not to lean so much upon revelations which may be uttered and invented by an evil spirit." He then suggests the articles should be sent to Rome "for the peace and tranquillity of your conscience." Two abbots, Nicolas of Jumièges and Guillaume of Cormeilles, gave an extremely cautious and kindly judgment. They urged that she should be "charitably admonished" and that she should have explained to her the danger she was running. It does not appear at first sight that they believed in her revelations. And, as to her claim that she was not guilty of mortal sin, "God alone knows, who reads the hearts of men." They end by saying that as they "were not present at her examination," they wanted to refer the matter to more eminent theologians.

The condemnation of Joan was far from unanimous, and this seems to have had some effect, for on April 18, Cauchon, accompanied by seven other priests, visited her to try "to lead her back to the path of truth and to a sincere profession of the Faith."

It is very difficult for us, so far away in time, to be sure of what was in the minds of these men. When we come to the last days of her life, it seems clear that she was tricked into an act which made her death inevitable and yet, until then, one cannot escape the impression that there were moments when her judges and prosecutors genuinely sought to save her. Few men are wholly bad, and these priests were not evil by any standards. They were, of course, fifteenth-century priests, molded in the patterns of thought and feeling of their day. Their beliefs were strong, so their tolerance was correspondingly very limited. Also, they were involved in politics, not the tame politics of a parliamentary democracy, but those of the sword. Yet they were not cruel, or at least no more cruel than those who administer the law today. We must not look at the past through modern lenses. Pontius Pilate was not a cruel man, nor was Cauchon. They were no more cruel than a British

Home Secretary or an American state governor who refuses to reprieve a criminal condemned to death. We must not be prejudiced by the manner of Joan's death: the stake, in that century, was no more and no less cruel a form of execution than the gallows, the electric chairs, and the cyanide eggs in this. They are all probably equally barbarous.

I think it is fair to assume that at least three quarters of the men concerned with Joan's trial were honestly convinced of her guilt and that most of those seventy-five per cent were anxious that she should, by repentance, save her soul—and so her body. The saving of her body, though important, was a very secondary matter. Joan and her judges were in agreement on that. Throughout the trial there seems to have been a swaying to and fro of feeling toward her, and on that day—April 18—I feel that the tide of emotion ran strongly in her favor. It is, of course, possible that from the start of the proceedings Cauchon would have been satisfied with a verdict of guilty and her repentance and recantation. She would then have been discredited, the French victories attributed to the devil, and Charles presented to Europe as a pretender-king whose coronation was the work of a heretic and a witch. The English, it is true, wanted Joan dead, but it would not have been easy for them to dispose of her if the Rouen court had accepted her repentance. We know what was in her judges' minds only through official documents and they, as all history shows, far too often reveal nothing of the impulses and irrationalities that sway men; nor, indeed, do they often disclose the backstair intrigues, the tussles for power, the bribes and bargains that result in a decision. Yet, as I read what was said on that particular day, I feel that Cauchon and those with him were acting with honest feelings of good will toward Joan.

"We"—it is Cauchon speaking—"told Joan, who said she was ill, that we and the other priests were visiting her in all friendliness and charity to give her comfort and consolation. We told her that for many days she had been examined before many learned persons, that she had answered most serious and difficult questions on the Faith, that her answers had been varied and contradictory, that wise and learned men had examined them most carefully and had found dangerous stuff in them. However, as she was an ignorant and uneducated woman, we would provide her with men, both kind and learned, wise and honest, and they would instruct her. We then asked those priests with us to counsel Joan so that her body and soul might be saved. But if Joan preferred others, we would send for them so that they could advise her on what to do and believe. We emphasized that we were priests and, because of that, were wholly disposed to use every possible means of seeking the salvation of her soul and the safety of her body—such means as we should use to save ourselves and our nearest relatives. We should be glad to let her have every day men fitted to give her suitable instruction and we would do for her all that the Church is wont to do in such circumstances, for she never shuts the fold against the lamb seeking to return. We told Joan to pay heed to what we said and to accept our invitation, for we should be forced to abandon her if, trusting to her own ignorance, she ignored our words. She must recognize her danger, one from which we sought to save her with all our love and strength."

What is one to make of this exhortation? Are they the words of a hypocritical monster? I find it very hard to think so. We cannot, though, be sure.

Joan thanked Cauchon and said: "As I am so ill, I think I am in great danger of death, and so I ask to be allowed to make my confession, to receive the Body of my Saviour, and to be buried in consecrated ground."

The account goes on: "We told her that if she wanted to receive the Sacraments she must behave as a good Catholic and submit to the Church. If she persisted in refusing to submit, she would not be allowed to receive the Sacraments, save that of penance, which we were always ready to administer. We told her that the more afraid she was of dying because of her illness, the more earnestly she ought to amend her life. We exhorted her to follow our counsel and asked her if she would submit to the Church Militant. She declared, 'No matter what happens to me, I will do and say nothing except what I have already said and done in my trial.' We finally told her that if she did not submit to the Church she would be abandoned as an infidel. Her answer was, 'I am a good Christian. I have been properly baptized and so I shall die a good Christian. I love God and want to support the Church with all my strength.'"

Cauchon made a final effort, a rather moving effort, as if he were trying to make a naughty little girl promise to be good by offering her a grand party. "We asked if she would not like to have a fine and splendid procession arranged to restore her to the Church. She said, 'I greatly want the Church and Catholics to pray for me.'"

A fortnight went by and then, on May 2, another full session of the court was held. Cauchon addressed it. He described what had been done in an endeavor to restore Joan to the Church, declared that all had so far failed, and announced that he had appointed the archdeacon of Evreux, one Jean de Chatillon, a venerable theologian, to address to her a solemn and public admonition, "since perhaps your presence and your exhortations may persuade her to be humble and obedient and dissuade her from relying too much on her own opinion; if any one of you thinks there is anything he can say or do to help her, we beg him not to hesitate for a moment to speak either to us or to this assembly."

Once again we are forced to ask: is this a speech just for the record or does it show genuine concern for Joan's fate? And once again we cannot be quite sure.

Joan was led in and was urged by Jean de Chatillon to listen carefully to what he was about to say. She replied, "Read your book"—meaning the text of his discourse which he had in his hand—"and then I will answer you. I trust in God my Creator for everything. I love Him with all my heart. I trust in my Judge. He is the King of Heaven and of earth."

De Chatillon began by telling her that they all wanted to act toward her with mercy and charity but that she would be in grave danger if she persisted in her own views after their errors had been pointed out to her. He then moved on to the question of the Church Militant. He expounded its nature, spoke of the authority it derives from God, explained that it is governed by the Holy Spirit and that it can never fall into error, that every Catholic must submit all his acts and sayings to its judgment, and that no one, no matter what he experiences of apparitions and revelations, can withdraw from the judgment of the Church because of them. Our Lord never desired anyone to call himself subject to God alone. He gave into the hands of the priesthood the authority and power to know and judge all the deeds of the faithful. Those who flouted priests flouted God, and those who listened to them listened to God. He warned her that the Church cannot err or pass a false judgment, and he who denied this is a heretic and, by canon law, is liable to severe punishment.

To all this Joan answered, "I do believe in the Church on earth but, as I have already declared, as far as what I have done and said are concerned I trust in God and refer myself to Him. I believe that the Church Militant cannot err or fail, but I submit all my words and deeds to God, Who caused me to do what I have done. I will say no more to you. And if I saw the fire waiting for me, I should still say what I have just said and nothing more."

The old archdeacon next turned to the matter of her dress, which he called indecent, scandalous, and against all virtue and custom. To show obstinacy by persisting in wearing it against the commandments of God and His apostles and the teachings of the Church was to stray from the Faith and fall into heresy. Joan said, as she had said before, that she would gladly put on a dress to go to church and receive the Blessed Sacrament, provided that immediately after her return she would be allowed to put on her present garment. She declared, "When I have finished what God sent me to do, I will resume woman's dress." The archdeacon asked if she really thought she was doing the right thing by wearing man's clothing. She replied, "I refer myself to Our Lord."

Her revelations were then attacked and discredited. They were branded as inventions and the root of all her many other crimes.

Joan gave strange answers to two of the questions put to her. One of them is quite meaningless. The first question was: "If we allow three or four priests of your own party to visit you, will you put before them the answers you've given in your trial and be guided by what they say?" Her answer was: "First

let them come and then I will answer." The second question
was: "Will you refer your behavior and submit yourself to the
clerics of Poitiers who originally examined you?" She said,
"Do you think you can trap me like that and make me yours?"
The meaning of this I cannot attempt to guess. Many biographers of Joan do not even record this answer. It is hard to
blame them, for it is quite incomprehensible. What possible
trap could there be in submitting to the judgment of men who
had long ago decided in her favor? Had Joan become so sus-
picious—it is not surprising—that she saw a snare in everything? Her answer to the first question can be understood, but
it remains a silly answer. Why did she not promise that she
would let priests of her own party judge her? It is true,
perhaps, that Cauchon had no intention of granting a safe-
conduct to any priests of the French party, but, on the other
hand, he may have been willing to. What had Joan to lose
by accepting his offer? I can only think that she was still ill or
suffering from the aftereffects of illness and that the strain of
the long trial and the conditions of her imprisonment were
beginning to tell heavily on her.

Finally, she was once again warned that her soul was in
great danger of eternal fire and her body of the fire of the stake.
And in turn she warned her judges, "You will not do as you
say against me without evil befalling you in body and soul."
She was taken back to her cell.

A week later, on May 9, her jailers led her to the torture
chamber of the castle. The instruments of torture were laid
out before her. Standing by them were the men ready to apply
them to her, "in order to restore her to the way and knowledge
of the truth and so achieve the salvation of her body and soul
which she so gravely endangered by her lies." Joan was un-

moved. She said, "Truly, if you were to tear my limbs apart and drive my soul from my body, I could not say anything different; and, if I did, I should declare afterward that you had made me say it by force." Her firmness saved her, "because of the hardness of her heart and the manner of her answering, we, her judges, feared that torture would not benefit her, so we decided not to apply it until we had taken further advice on the matter." A dozen of the assessors gathered in the bishop's palace three days later to settle the question of whether or not to torture Joan. After much talk, three of them voted in favor of torturing her. The rest voted against. So the minutes of the meeting noted that "it was neither necessary nor expedient to submit her to the torture."

A week after this decision was taken, the verdict of the University of Paris was delivered. Cauchon had sent the twelve articles which the clerics of Rouen had considered, for a condemnation by Paris would carry immeasurably more weight throughout Christendom than anything Rouen could say. The university had no doubt about Joan's iniquity and did not mince its words. Her revelations, it declared, were "fictitious and pernicious lies, inspired by diabolical spirits such as Satan, Belial, and Behemoth"; Joan herself was "blasphemous, cunning, cruel, and seditious, a wanderer from the Faith, schismatic and apostate, a liar and a witch."

On May 23, exactly a year since she was captured at Compiègne, Joan was again brought before her judges. It should be noted that it was three weeks since she had last seen them, three weeks since she had left her cell, except for the short visit to the torture chamber. She had lived through five hundred hours in the half-light of her prison, never alone, always in the presence of her barbarous jailers, and deprived of the infinite consolation of the Mass and the Blessed Sacrament. This long spell of unbroken restraint came at the end of eleven months' captivity. It may account for what happened the next day.

May 22 brought her trial to an end. She had read to her again the charges leveled against her and he was condemned on each one. A last appeal was then made, delivered this time by Pierre Maurice, a canon of Rouen and a celebrated doctor of theology. He began by saying, "Dear Joan, the time has come for you to think most carefully over all that has been said," and he begged her not to choose "the way of eternal damnation." He was a man of sense, for he then went on to appeal to her by setting the matter within a military framework, obviously hoping it would help her to see the enormity of her attitude. He said, "Suppose your King had told you to defend one of his fortresses and on no account to let anyone enter. Surely, in that case, you would refuse to admit someone who claimed to be sent by the King but had no letters or sign from him to prove the truth of his claim. Now, Our Lord, when He ascended into heaven, gave the government of the Church to St. Peter and his successors. He forbade them to receive those who claimed to come in His name but who gave no proof and had no sign other than their own protestations. And so you should not have had any trust in those you say visited you, and we should not believe in you, since to do so is contrary to God's command. And, Joan, you should also consider this: if when you were serving your King one of his soldiers had declared that he would obey neither the King nor any of his captains, you would, I am certain, have said that he was to be condemned. So what have you to say about yourself, a Christian, if you refuse to obey Christ's officers who are the prelates of the Church?"

He ended with a vehement exhortation: "Obey the Church and submit to its judgment. If you will not, if you continue in error, your soul will be damned and your body destroyed. Do not be held back by human pride and false shame, nor because you fear that by submitting you will lose the great honors you have had. The honor of God and your salvation come before all. You will lose everything if you do not do as I say. I beg and implore you, by the pity you have for the passion of Christ and by the love you must have for your body and soul, to correct your errors and return to the truth. This you can do by obedience to the Church and by submitting in all things to her judgment. Thus you will save your soul and snatch back your body from death. If not—as I have already said—your soul will be swept away to eternal damnation and your body will be burned. May Our Lord preserve you from such an end!"

Strong words, to which Joan replied, "as to what I have said and done, I stand by it all. If at this moment I saw the stake with the faggots alight and if I were in the flames, I would still say what I have said," In the margin of the court record, one of the notaries scribbled, *responsio superba,*—"an arrogant reply."

With that, the trial ended. Next day was appointed as that on which sentence would be pronounced.

It was Thursday, May 24. Early in the morning Joan was placed in a cart and, with a strong escort of soldiers, taken to the cemetery of the Abbey of Saint-Ouen, one of the great churches of Rouen. It was a well-known place, for on the feast day of the saint a big and popular fair was held there every year. A great crowd had assembled by the time Joan arrived, made up of English soldiers and French civilians. Against the wall of the church a big wooden stand had been erected. On it were seated Cauchon, the Cardinal of Winchester, three bishops—those of Therouanne, Noyon, and Norwich—seven abbots, two priors, and a host of lesser fry. Facing it was a much smaller stand, rather like a large pulpit. Joan was led up into it and was followed by Canon Guillaume Erard, who had been chosen to preach the final sermon. He chose as his text a verse from St. John's Gospel: "The branch cannot bear fruit of itself, unless it abide on the vine." He said the same kind of thing that Joan had already heard a dozen times, but at one point he faced Joan and burst out with, "How terribly, France, have you been deceived! Once you were the most Christian of all nations, but this Charles, who pretends to be your King, has, in the manner of a heretic and schismatic, put his trust in the words and deeds of an infamous and dishonorable woman. Yes, Joan, it is you I mean, and I tell you that your King is a heretic and schismatic."

Joan instantly sprang to life. She cried, "Most reverend sir, I tell you and will swear and stake my life that he is the noblest of all Christians and that there is no one who has a greater love for religion and the Church. He is nothing like what you say he is." One wonders if these words were reported to Charles? Did he weep? Did he regret that he had never raised a finger to save her?

Erard finished his sermon with a final demand that she make her submission. Joan replied, "Let all that I have said and done be sent to Rome to our Holy Father the Pope to whom, after God, I refer myself. All that I have said and done was at God's command." She was promptly told that the Pope was too far away to be consulted and that each bishop in his diocese was a competent judge. Three formal and separate admonitions were then delivered. Now here I transcribe what was set down in the official report of her trial:

"As she would say no more, we, the Bishop of Beauvais, began to read the sentence. We had nearly finished, when Joan interrupted us and said she would hold fast to all that the Church ordained and to all that her judges decreed and that she would obey us in everything. She repeated again and again that, as learned clerics had declared her revelations and apparitions were not to be believed, she would no longer have faith in them, but would in all things submit to her judges and the Church. Then, in our presence and before a great multitude of spectators, she recanted and abjured her past sins, using the words of a document drawn up in French. She read it and signed it with her own hand. Here follows the text of the abjurations:

" 'Those who have wandered from the Christian faith and have, through the grace of God, returned to the truth and to Holy Mother Church should strive to prevent Satan from ensnaring them again and causing them to fall again into error and damnation. So it is that I, Joan, known as the Maid, now realize the errors in which I was enmeshed and, having through God's grace, been brought back to our Holy Mother Church, confess that I have greatly sinned. I do this to make plain that my return to the Church is not feigned, that I have come back willingly. I have falsely pretended that I have had revelations from God and that His angels and St. Catherine and St. Margaret have appeared to me; I have seduced others into foolish and wrong beliefs; I have made superstitious divinations; I have blasphemed God and His saints; I have broken the laws of God, Holy Scripture, and canon law; I have worn immodest dress against the decent order of nature and have had my hair cropped like a man's against all womanly modesty; I have borne arms presumptuously and I have cruelly desired to shed blood; I declared that all this was done at the command of God, His angels and His saints; I have been both seditious and idolatrous and have summoned and adored evil spirits. I also confess that I have been schismatic and in countless ways have strayed from the truth. By God's grace and because of the sound doctrine and counsel which you and the other doctors put before me, I now most sincerely abjure and recant these crimes and errors and renounce and separate myself from all of them. I submit myself wholly and completely to the correction of our Holy Mother Church and your justice. Moreover, I vow, swear, and promise to St. Peter, Prince of the Apostles, to our Holy Father the Pope and his successors, and to you, the Bishop of Beauvais and the religious brother, Jean le Maistre, vicar of the Lord Inquisitor of the Faith who are my judges, that I will never return to these errors from which God has delivered me, but that I will always dwell in the unity of our Holy Mother Church and in the obedience of our Holy Father the Pope of Rome. This I swear by God Almighty and by the Holy Gospels, and I have signed this abjuration with my mark.'"

The Bishop then pronounced sentence. The important words were these: "After being repeatedly admonished with all charity, you have, after much delay, been enabled by God's help to return to the bosom of our Holy Mother Church. We believe that, with a truly contrite heart, you have genuinely renounced your errors and, as you have publicly abjured them and all heresy, we remove from you the bonds of excommunication in which you were chained—provided that you return to the Church in all sincerity and determined to obey all that we shall command. For, because you have rashly sinned against God and the Church, we condemn you to the salutary penance of perpetual imprisonment with the bread of sorrow and the water of affliction, that you may weep for your sins and never again do anything to cause fresh tears."

What are we to think of this? There is nothing psychologically impossible in Joan's making such an adjuration. It is, admittedly, a most abject document in which she abandons every position and denies everything for which she has fought, faced torture and death. But she had been a prisoner for a year, for three hundred and sixty-five days and nights, and since her arrival in Rouen she had never once been allowed out into the open air. She had been ill, many of her nights must have been sleepless, she had attended no Mass, she had been questioned and questioned and questioned, entreated, beseeched, and threatened. Nothing had been spared in the efforts to brainwash her. Then suddenly she was taken into the midst of a vast, noisy crowd. The noise, the light, and the color must have stunned her. She had in prison often been threatened with the stake, but on this bright May morning she could look down and see the red-clothed executioner and his assistants waiting for her. What had been a matter of words suddenly and horribly became very real and very near. If she failed to submit there and then, her body would feel the flames within an hour. She was only nineteen, so it would not be surprising if her spirit broke and she signed a recantation as complete and abject as those wrung from so many political prisoners of our own day.

It is, however, almost certain that she did not sign this document of abjuration, that she did not even know of its existence. For a few moments there was great confusion around her and it is impossible to know exactly what happened. From evidence

I shall quote it is, though, nearly certain that, although she signed something, it was not the document which appeared in the official report. It is one more example among the myriad which history provides of the great truth, valid at all times and in all countries, that state papers are highly suspect; that, at best, they present a one-sided account of affairs; and that, far too often, they are propaganda sheets with deception as their prime purpose. So let us ignore the report and see what others, besides Cauchon, who were present have to say.

As Cauchon began to read the condemnation, several of the priests and notaries around Joan pleaded urgently with her to yield. "Joan, we are full of pity for you . . . recant, or you will be burned . . . say you'll dress like a woman . . . do as we say, and you'll be let out of prison." Joan was heard to exclaim, "How you tire yourselves trying to make me give in!" And one man, Guillaume Manchon, the chief notary at the trial, said that Joan finally answered "that she was ready to obey the Church." There was, most obviously, a scene of tremendous chaos, with people milling to and fro, pleading, arguing, and shouting—and some of them throwing stones. The upshot of it all was that Joan signed something. The most important witness is Jean Massieu, one of the ushers. He says: "Guillaume Erard produced a declaration of abjuration and handed it to me to read to her. I read it and remember very well that it said she must never carry arms again, that she must not wear men's clothing and cut her hair short. There were one or two other things I've forgotten. But I am quite certain that the document was only eight lines long and I am just as certain that it is not the one given in the official report. The one I read to Joan was quite different from that given in the report, and it was the one I read that Joan signed. I am very sure of that."

Here are four more witnesses. A clerk, one Taguel, says: "I well remember watching Joan when the abjuration document was read to her by Jean Massieu. It was in French and there were about six lines of large writing." Another clerk, Guillaume de la Chambre, declares: "The thing she signed was a piece of paper containing six or seven lines of writing." And the Bishop of Noyon says: "It was quite evident that Joan paid little attention to the recantation and did not understand it." Jean Monnet, too, also swears that it was a document of only six or seven lines.

One other point: Joan laughed as she signed this document of seven or eight lines.

So we must, I think, believe that what Joan signed was what Massieu remembered it to have been: a brief promise to wear women's clothes and not bear arms again. In return, her life was to be spared and she was to be placed in a prison under the control of the Church. Her signing of this scrap of paper displeased the English. One of their theologians, noticing her laugh as she signed, told Cauchon he was wrong in accepting her repentance and that she was mocking them all. Cauchon's temper flared. He called the Englishman a liar and said, "She was tried for heresy, and it has been my duty to work for her salvation rather than her death"—a strange remark if we accept the view that Cauchon would use any trick, however foul, to secure her execution.

A lay lawyer, Jean Fave, says: "From all I heard, the English were furious with the Bishop of Beauvais and with the doctors and all the others concerned in the case because Joan was not found guilty and handed over to the executioners. It was said they were so angry that they drew their swords against the bishop and other clergy as they walked back to the castle, shouting: 'The King has wasted his money on you.' But they did not touch them. I have heard it said also that the Earl of Warwick stopped the bishop and others and complained that things were going badly for the King and that Joan had slipped out of the English hands. One of them replied: 'There is nothing to worry about, my lord, we shall catch her yet.'"

When Joan had put her mark at the foot of the paper offered her, Loiseleur, the priest who in her early days in prison had tricked her into confiding in him, sidled up to her and said, "Thank God, Joan, that you have done a good day's work and saved your soul." "And now," she replied, "will you clerics take me to one of your prisons, so that I shall be out of the hands of the English?" Cauchon intervened with, "Take her back whence you brought her." And back she was taken to her cell in the castle.

Once again we come up against the question: just what was Cauchon's game? Was this order of his the product of villainy, cunning, or weakness? I cannot believe that, throughout the trial, he remained adamant that Joan must die. At the start of the proceedings, it seems that he was so determined but, as the days went by, Joan's personality very obviously affected him and his resolution weakened. Again I cannot believe that all his exhortations and appeals were made tongue in cheek. For had Joan yielded much earlier and submitted in open court before the end of the trial, it would have been almost impossible to execute her. The scandal would have blazed across Christendom. He was, though, a frightened and ambitious man, and it must have seemed to him that his ambitions could be realized only by placating the English. Certainly no physical harm would have come to him had he defied them, but though the Church was powerful enough to save him from physical moles-

tation, it could not—and its local representatives would not—
have saved him from being stripped of wealth and power. From
time to time he fell under the spell of Joan, but he lived with
and among the English and they cast a more powerful spell on
him, one compounded of fear and greed. It is the only explanation of the frequent swing of his attitude toward her. In this
particular instance he very probably meant to send Joan to a
prison of the Church, but the moment the English heard
sentence passed on her and realized she had escaped death, an
angry tumult broke out. Cauchon lost his nerve and ordered
her back into English keeping.

Later that day Joan put on women's clothes and allowed her
head to be shaved, to remove all trace of her masculine haircut.
That was on Thursday. On the following Sunday she was
again dressed as a man. A rumor reached her judges on the
day following her re-entry into prison that she had already begun to regret having assumed women's clothes, so Cauchon
sent Jean Beaupère, one of the University of Paris' representatives at the trial, together with another priest, Nicolas Midy,
to speak with her and urge her to continue along the right path
and warn her of the fatal and immediate consequences of a
relapse. When they arrived in the courtyard of the castle they
found some Englishmen there. They were Englishmen in a
nasty mood, and as soon as they caught sight of the two French
priests they began saying loud and clear that a good job would
be done if someone threw them both into the river. Beaupère
and Midy promptly turned and walked back over the castle
bridge, where they met another group of English, who also
suggested they would be better in the river. Beaupère says:
"This terrified us and we left the castle without speaking to
Joan."

The rumor that she wanted to revert to men's clothing seems to have been only a rumor, but it is a fact that she did put on the forbidden clothes, and Jean Massieu tells how it happened. "On the following Sunday morning, she said to her English guard when it was time for her to get up, 'Unfasten my chains, I'm going to get up.' One of the Englishmen grabbed her women's clothes and took the sack in which her male garments had been put. He shook them out, flung them at her, and stowed her women's clothes in the sack. Joan said, 'You know I am forbidden to wear the garments of a man—and I won't wear them.' But they would not give her any other clothes, and the argument about them went on until midday. Finally her physical needs forced her to get up and go out, so she had to wear the men's clothes. When she came back, the guards refused to give her back her women's clothes, though she begged and pleaded with them."

There is another reason given for her action. One priest, Martin Ladvenu, says: "I heard from Joan herself that a great English lord entered her cell and tried to rape her. That was why, she said, she had resumed male clothes." But Massieu, our previous witness, also said he had the story from Joan's own lips and he makes no mention of rape. Another man, Pierre Cusquel, declares: "People said the sole cause of her condemnation was that she had resumed male clothes and that she would not have done so except to prevent the advances of the soldiers with whom she lived. I asked her why she wore these male clothes, and that was her answer."

On Monday, Cauchon, with eight companions, visited Joan. The official report says: "Because Joan was wearing a man's dress, a short mantle, a hood, and a doublet, we questioned her to find out when and why she had resumed a man's dress and rejected women's clothes. She said she had only recently resumed man's dress and declared, 'I have resumed it of my own free will and no one has compelled me to. I prefer the clothes of a man to those of a woman.'"

So we have three reasons given for this fatal step: she was tricked into it by her guards, she took it to protect her virginity, she made it freely and deliberately. Once again the official report lies. One of the companions of Cauchon was Friar Isambard, and he was to testify later: "When she had put on male clothes again, she excused herself before us. She said that when she began wearing women's clothes the English had treated her shamefully and violently. And she was weeping as she spoke, with tears streaming down her face, and she looked so outraged and disfigured that I felt the deepest pity for her." There is not a word of this in the report.

It goes on to record the rest of the questioning, and we can fairly safely accept it as accurate, because it is never contradicted by the men who were there and later gave evidence at the rehabilitation process. It is also supported by Joan's words and attitude on the day she died. The report says: "She was asked if she had not sworn never to wear male costume again and answered, 'I would rather die then remain in chains, but if I can go to Mass and be put in a decent prison with a woman as a companion, I will be good and obey the Church.' We then asked if she had again heard the voices of St. Catherine and St. Margaret. She said she had and she told us what they had said: 'They told me that, through them, God declared His grief that I had behaved like a traitor by consenting to recant in order to save my life; by saving my life I was damning myself. Before last Thursday, my voices told me what I should do and I did it. And on Thursday, while the priest was preaching, my voices told me to answer him boldly. He was a false preacher and accused me of many things I had not done. If I were to declare that God had not sent me, I should damn myself, for it is true that God did send me. Ever since Thursday my voices have told me that I had behaved very wickedly in saying that what I did was wrong. What I said last Thursday, I said only because I was frightened of the stake. Now I would rather die than stay in this prison. If you want me to I will put on women's clothes again, but I will do nothing else." Against the opening words of her statement—"They told me that, through them, God declared . . ." The clerk taking them down wrote in the margin *responsio mortifera*—a fatal answer—as indeed it was. When Cauchon left the castle he met the Earl of Warwick and a little group of Englishmen. He said to them, "Farewell! Farewell! It is done. Be of good cheer." These words are always taken to mean that Cauchon was well satisfied that his plotting against Joan had at last succeeded. They are read as an exclamation of triumph. That is not at all the way I understand them. To me, it is a bitter, contemptuous remark, the remark of a man telling his masters that they can now relax, for their dirty work has been done for them. But there is neither pride nor triumph in it.

The next day, forty-one of the assessors met in the archepiscopal chapel. Cauchon told them what Joan had said and asked for their opinion. Each of them was of the same mind: she was a "relapsed heretic." Nothing could save her from the fire.

So we come to Wednesday, May 30, 1431. Massieu saw Joan in her cell early that morning and told her she would be taken to the Old Market Place at eight o'clock to have her new sentence passed upon her. Two monks also arrived, Martin

Ladvenu and Jean Toutmouille, to prepare her for death. Ladvenu told her how she was to die. She had, of course, always known that the stake was the penalty for a relapsed heretic, but the knowledge that the fire was only an hour or two away made her burst into tears. She cried, "Oh! That I should be treated so cruelly! Oh! That my pure and unblemished body, which has never been defiled, must today be burned to ashes! I'd rather have my head cut off seven times than be burned like this. I should not have come to this wretched end if only I had been in the hands of the Church instead of being held by my enemies. I call on God, the supreme Judge, to note the great wrong that is being done me."

At that moment Cauchon entered. She turned to him and exclaimed, "My Lord Bishop, I die because of you."

"No, Joan," he told her, "you are to die because you did not keep your promise to us and because you returned to your former sin."

Again she said, "If you had only put me in a prison of the Church and let me be looked after by decent and proper warders, this would never have happened. And so I appeal to God against you."

With Cauchon was one of the assessors, Pierre Maurice. Joan asked him, "Where shall I be tonight?"

"Have you no trust in God?"

"Yes, and by His grace I shall be in Paradise."

Cauchon left the cell. Ladvenu had heard her confession earlier. He sent Massieu after Cauchon to ask his permission to give her Holy Communion. Cauchon said: "Give It to her and anything else she asks for." Again, another strange remark to come from him. He knew she had confessed, but he must have realized that she would not have confessed to being a heretic. Therefore, she was in a state of mortal sin and so could not be allowed to consume the Body of Christ. So why did Cauchon give permission for her to have Communion? Was it because he knew in his heart that she was no heretic but the innocent victim of the State?

Joan was led from the castle, wearing a long robe. She was placed in a cart and, escorted by a strong guard of English soldiers, was taken to the Old Market Place. An enormous crowd awaited her. Spectators were jammed in every window. Two platforms had been raised in the square, one for Joan, the other for the dignitaries of Church and State. In the very center of the square was a more sinister erection: a plaster stake with a pile of faggots heaped around its base. Joan mounted her platform. "For her salutary admonition and the edification of the people, a solemn sermon was preached by the distinguished theologian, Master Nicolas Midy. He took as his text the words of the Apostle in the twelfth chapter of the first epistle to the Corinthians: 'And if one member suffer any thing, all the members suffer with it.'" He ended his sermon with: "Joan, go in peace. The Church can no longer defend you, but surrenders you into the hands of the secular authorities."

Throughout the sermon Joan prayed. Massieu and Ladvenu, the two priests who stayed with her to the end, recount that she invoked the Holy Trinity, the Blessed Virgin, and all the saints of Paradise. She also gazed down on the crowd and cried, "I beg all of you standing there to forgive any harm I have done, so as I forgive you the harm you have done me, I beseech you to pray for me." And to the priests she saw standing there she said, "Please say a Mass for me." She prayed for at least half an hour after the sermon had ended; "almost every-

one who was there wept for pity—even some of the English."
But, no matter how copiously the tears flowed, the final,
irrevocable sentence was delivered by Cauchon: "We declare
that you have fallen again into your former errors and we decree
that you are a relapsed heretic. We condemn you as a rotten
member and, in order that you may not infect the other members of Christ, you must be cast out of the unity of the Church,
cut off from her, and delivered to the secular power. We cast
you off and abandon you, praying that the secular power will
be moderate in its judgment toward you."

Joan asked to be given a cross. An English soldier heard her,
quickly fashioned one—a very small one—from two bits of
wood, and handed it to her; "she kissed it most devoutly as
she took it and put it against her breast, between her flesh and
her gown." But others among the English were getting im-
patient and began shouting, "Do you priests mean to keep us till
dinnertime?" She was led down from her platform and taken
before the one on which sat the magistrates. The chief one, who
should have formally condemned and sentenced her, merely
waved his hand and said, "Take her!"

She was led to the stake. A paper cap was put on her head.
In large letters it bore the words: "Heretic, Relapsed Sinner,
Apostate, Idolater." She asked Massieu to fetch her a crucifix.
He ran to the nearby church, tore one off its wall, and she knelt
and kissed it at the foot of the stake. She mounted the heap
of faggots, and the executioner chained her to the pillar. "As
they were fastening her, she implored the help of St. Michael,"
a witness records, and Ladvenu says, "She maintained at the
very end that the voices she had heard came from God and that
everything she had done had been done at God's command.
She said her voices had not deceived her and that the revela-

tions she had had were from God." As she was left alone, waiting for the flames, she cried down to Massieu, "Hold the crucifix up so that I can see it the whole time."

By then all the representatives of the Church, except the handful of priests by the stake, had left the square, too afraid to witness what they had made inevitable.

The executioner lit the pyre. "When Joan saw the fire set to the wood, she began to cry aloud, 'Jesus! Jesus!' and she went on crying 'Jesus!' until she died. On English orders, the executioner pulled aside the blazing wood so that the spectators could see her charred and naked body hanging there and be certain she was dead. He threw more faggots on the fire, along with oil and sulphur, but he said that neither her heart nor her intestines would burn away. When the fire had died down, all that remained of her was gathered together and thrown in the Seine.

Nearly everyone who was present felt they had witnessed a great crime. There was, for example, an English soldier well known for his detestation of Joan. For weeks he had been boasting that he would lay a faggot of his own on her pyre. He did, but when he heard her cries of "Jesus!" he was seized with horror and collapsed. He was taken to a nearby tavern and given wine. After he had come to his senses, he sought out a Dominican friar, another Englishman, and confessed to him that he had committed a most grievous sin and that he thought Joan was a saint.

Another Englishman, John Tressart, secretary to the King of England, was weeping as he walked away and told his friends, "We are all lost, for we have burned a saint." A canon of Rouen, Jean Alepée, sobbed: "Would that my soul were now where I believe hers to be." Manchon, the notary, declared,

"I never wept as much and could not stop weeping whenever I thought of her for a whole month after she was burned. With some of the money I was paid for my work in the case, I bought a little missal to remind me to pray for her."

Even the executioner hurried to the Dominicans and declared that he thought he was damned because he had burned a saint.

That afternoon and evening, Rouen was a hushed, subdued town. The taverns were full, as usual, but so were the churches, and there were little groups of people at every corner. Over all there seemed to hang the smell of burning flesh.

With Joan's death, the way seemed clear for the English to resume their onslaught upon France and sweep to final victory. But it did not happen like that.

In December of that year the King of England was crowned King of France, but not at Rheims. The ceremony took place in Notre-Dame in Paris and it was a mean and shabby affair. It did nothing to extend the English power. The Duke of Bedford's wife died. She was the Duke of Burgundy's sister. Bedford married again rather hastily, and Burgundy considered this a slight to his sister's memory. A coolness sprang up between the two old allies. In August, 1435, the Congress of Arras was held, at which England, Burgundy, and France met in an attempt to end the war. It failed. The French asked England to renounce forever the title of King of France for her own kings; in return, she could retain almost all Normandy and the kingdom of Guyenne. They were generous terms, but the English rejected them and, at the end of the year, Burgundy and France allied themselves to drive the English out. In the spring of the following year, French troops entered Paris. Rouen was reconquered in 1449; Dunois, the friend and companion-in-arms of Joan, was there to watch the English garrison ride out. Soon, only Guyenne was left to the English. On June 17, 1452, the town of Castillon, on the Dordogne, was besieged by the French. An English army, commanded by the Earl of Shrewsbury, the famous Talbot who had fought at Orléans against Joan, was sent to its relief. The French won an easy victory and Talbot, badly wounded, died on the field. He was sixty-three; nearly fifty of those years had been spent in fighting the French. Four months later, on October 19, Bordeaux surrendered. The Hundred Years' War was over and the English were out of France.

7. The Vindication

MEANWHILE, what of Joan? Was she a day's wonder, now forgotten? Far from it. Prayers were said for her, poems written about her, and her name continued to inspire the soldiers of France. Many people rejoiced that "all those who were guilty of her death died most shamefully." Cauchon fell back dead as his barber was trimming his beard; d'Estivet's body was found in a gutter; Nicolas Midy was stricken with leprosy and died in a lazar house.

And Charles, at long last, bestirred himself. He had succeeded in winning back his kingdom, and success is all that matters to the world when the affairs of state are involved; but, although realizing this, he was a little uneasy at having it on record that he owed his crown to a condemned and executed heretic and witch. He wanted that stain removed. It would, though, be unfair not to recognize that he also wanted to restore Joan's reputation for Joan's sake. He had made no effort to save her while she was alive, but then he was weak, irresolute, and a coward, the nominal head of a torn and divided kingdom. These facts explain, though they do not excuse, his inaction. A modern apologist for him says he pretended to have no interest in Joan because he wanted to get hold of all the documents about the trial. They were in Rouen. To have announced that he was deeply concerned to reverse the verdict on her would have meant that the English either took those documents to England or destroyed them. Perhaps. It is an ingenious theory and certainly Charles acted two or three months after Rouen fell to him.

However, that is only a theory. The fact is that as the English were driven to the sea, as the years brought him experience, and as his throne grew secure and strong his character changed. He became confident and determined, able to decide and act, and one of his decisions was that the time had come for him to rehabilitate Joan. No decree of his could effect this. An ecclesiastical court had condemned her; an ecclesiastical court must restore her good fame. In February, 1449, Charles declared that Joan had been "executed unjustly, most cruelly, and against reason," and he ordered Guillaume Bouille, an eminent theologian and one of his counselors, to find out "the truth about the trial and the way it was conducted." Bouille interviewed a few of the men who had taken part in the trial, and from what they told him he drew up a statement which he submitted to a small group of lawyers and theologians. On the basis of that statement, they declared the trial to have been invalid. The constitution of the court was illegal, its proceedings irregular, and its verdict wrong—all of which made very pleasant and welcome hearing for Charles.

By itself, this declaration did nothing to clear Joan. It merely gave Charles good grounds for seeking a full, official, canonical reversal of the Rouen verdict. It was not until 1452 that he was able to seek this reversal. In the preceding year Pope Nicolas V sent a Norman to France as his legate. He was Guillaume d'Estouteville, who later became Archbishop of Rouen. The Pope was anxious to secure peace among the rulers of the West in face of the rapidly mounting threat from Islam, a threat that became sharp and near in May, 1453, when the Ottoman hordes overran the defenses of Constantinople and seized the great advance bastion of Christianity. The papal legate in France was instructed to sound Charles about the possibility of his joining another crusade against the infidel. He made it evident that he, for his part, was willing to examine sympathetically the question of restoring the good name of Joan. For if the Pope could legitimately overturn the verdict passed by the Rouen court, Charles would, it was thought, inevitably by prepared to listen with greater interest to papal suggestions for a crusade. D'Estouteville was, too, a good Frenchman who genuinely believed that Charles was the true and legitimate King of France and, as a patriot, would be glad to see the stain upon his King removed. So soon after his arrival in France he approached the Grand Inquisitor of France, Jean Brehal, a Dominican, and the two of them went to Rouen and summoned a variety of witnesses.

The evidence they heard made them draw up a document which consisted of twenty-seven articles, each of which dealt with an aspect of Joan's imprisonment, trial, and condemnation. The whole document declared plainly and bluntly that she had been most wrongly treated, that the court proceedings were rigged, and that she had lived a holy and Catholic life. The following year the Grand Inquisitor visited Rome "concerning the case of the late Joan the Maid." Nicolas V was not an outstandingly courageous Pope. His legate in France wanted to please Charles. So also did Nicolas, but he realized that pleasing Charles in the matter of Joan would enrage the English. So it was decided that any move toward Joan's rehabilitation should not appear to be taken at the instigation of the French King and, from a State affair, it was turned into a private matter.

Joan's mother, Isabelle Romée, and her two brothers, Pierre and Jean, were still alive. They had left Domrémy and lived in Orléans in enjoyment of a pension from that always-grateful town. Isabelle was persuaded to put forward a petition for the reversal of the verdict on her daughter. Death prevented Pope Nicolas from having to do anything about this petition. His successor was a Borgia, Calixtus III. He acted quickly. In June, 1455, just over two months after his accession, he authorized the opening of proceedings and appointed three commissioners to be in charge of them: the Archbishop of Rheims, the Bishop of Paris, and the Bishop of Coutances. In the past, all three men had been vigorous supporters of the cause of Charles VII.

The opening scene of these proceedings took place in Paris in the Cathedral of Notre-Dame on November 7, 1455. The papal commissioners, accompanied by the Grand Inquisitor, took their seats in the nave. Then Isabelle, supported by her two sons, by priests and a crowd of lay people from Orléans, entered, uttering "great sighs and groans" and made "pitiful plaints and supplications." She handed the papal order to the commissioners, and a great wave of emotion swept through the cathedral, which by then was crammed to the door with spectators. There were shouts and tears; some began chanting, others prayed aloud, and Isabelle had to be hurried into the sacristy to avoid being mobbed.

That was the formal opening of the process which was to vindicate Joan. The real business began on November 17, in the audience chamber of the Bishop of Paris, before a formidable array of prelates. Witness after witness stepped forward and gave evidence on Joan's stay at Chinon, her activities in the field, her life in prison, and her trial. Toward the middle of December the investigation moved to Rouen, where fresh witnesses were heard, and it was there that the discovery was made of facts which at once invalidated Joan's trial.

Guillaume Manchon, one of the three notaries, said in reply

to questions: "During the first few days of the trial, when I was keeping a record of what Joan said, the judges tried to make me alter her words when I translated them into Latin and so change the sense of her statements. At the Bishop of Beauvais' orders, two men were placed in a window alcove near the judges and a curtain was drawn in front of them so that no one in the body of the court knew they were there. Their job was to write down everything that tended to make Joan seem guilty and to omit from their record anything that favored her. Their report and mine were compared after each session, and theirs was always quite different from mine—which annoyed the bishop very much." Manchon had his way, however, and he said that the final report he wrote was accurate. But the presence of the hidden men by the window showed the rehabilitation court the atmosphere prevailing at the original trial. The questioning of Manchon continued and produced a supremely damning fact. He was asked why the original seventy articles extracted from Joan's replies had been reduced to twelve. It will be remembered that it was by these twelve articles that Joan was condemned.

"It was decided," Manchon said, "that all the articles should be reduced to a few, so that their examination could be easily and quickly ended. But I did not reduce them, nor do I know who did." He was asked if the final twelve articles were read to Joan. His answer was "No." Another question put to him was: "Did you notice that the articles were very different from Joan's actual replies?" He said, "I don't remember. The men who sent them to Paris said it was quite usual to make such extracts and I should not have dared to question such important people."

So the whole case against Joan was contained in a short

précis of a long document, a précis that omitted everything she had said in explanation and defense of her deeds.

The commissioners sent representatives to Domrémy to collect the evidence of those who knew Joan as a child, and they also went to Vaucouleurs. They finished their work by the middle of February. Other investigators, headed by the Archbishop of Rheims, went to Orléans. The hearing of the final witnesses was concluded at Rouen in May, and on June 10 every document was given to the Grand Inquisitor. From them he produced a closely reasoned study of the case, which he named the *Recollectio*. In it he examined with great thoroughness the charges brought against her and refuted them one by one. He then scrutinized the conduct of her trial, exposed all its irregularities, and destroyed once and for all any claim of the original Rouen court to be a competent judicial body. This *Recollectio* and the documents on which it was based were given to the papal commissioners, and at eight o'clock on the morning of July 7, 1456, the Archbishop of Rheims took his seat in the hall of the archepiscopal palace in Rouen. On one side of him was the Bishop of Paris, on the other the Bishop of Coutances. Behind them stood the Grand Inquisitor. Joan's brother, Jean, was present and the hall was crowded with the people of Rouen. One of them was Martin Ladvenu, the priest who had heard Joan's last confession. The archbishop gave the verdict of the commission: "We, from our seats of judgments and thinking only of God, say and decree that the trial and condemnation of the Maid was tainted with fraud, malice, and gross errors of fact and law and that this trial and condemnation, together with the abjuration and the execution and all their consequences, were and are null and void and are to be quashed."

The commission went in procession to the cemetery of Saint-Ouen, where the episode of the abjuration took place, and the judgment was read again. On the next day it was read on the spot where she had been executed, and there were processions in her honor in all the towns and cities of France.

More than four hundred years went by and then the city of Orléans, having lost none of its love for Joan, spoke through the person of its bishop, the famous Monseigneur Dupanloup. In 1869 he invited to the annual ceremony commemorating the raising of the siege the bishops of all the towns visited by Joan before her capture, and to them he made a most eloquent and memorable speech extolling the significance of Joan as a Catholic and as a patriot. The assembled bishops appealed to the Pope, Pius IX. They said: "It is the whole world, not only Orléans and France, which venerates the deeds of God accomplished through Joan of Arc. They admire and marvel at this young girl's piety, the complete devotion and forgetfulness of self with which she always carried out the will of God. And they have noted that holiness which she showed at Domrémy, where she looked after her father's cattle as a little peasant girl, on the battlefield where her ability and courage were those of a great captain, and at the stake, where she made manifest her unswerving loyalty to the Catholic faith and the Apostolic See. For long, the popes of Rome have defended and praised this heroine, and it is now the wish of the faithful that Your Holiness should show particular honor to her memory. Such honor would be a just tribute to the Maid who both freed her country and saved it from heresy. It would also honor the people of France, who have done so much for religion and for the throne of St. Peter."

In 1909, Pius X beatified her and in May, 1920, she was canonized by Benedict XV, exactly four hundred and eighty-nine years after the bright flames began to crackle around her in the market square of Rouen.

8. The Saint

THAT IRISH SERVANT of God, Matt Talbot, used to call St. Thérèse of the Child Jesus "a great girl," and I imagine that is how most of us think of St. Joan. We admire her courage, her strength of will, enjoy her dash and gaiety, rejoice in her triumphs on the battlefield, and feel profound respect and immense sorrow as we watch her burn. But a saint? She was a warrior girl who freed her country from foreign domination. So she is, very naturally, the national heroine of France and it is very natural that there should be ceremonies in her honor every year and that statues of her should be dotted about the squares of France. But a saint, someone whose life has a message as important to the English and the Americans and to the rest of the world as it is to the French?

We accept the fact that she is a saint because the Church says so. That is understood. But is it a rather grudging acceptance, or do we recognize her sanctity warmly and with our whole being? She left no scrap of spiritual doctrine behind; her life was marked by no great austerity nor any deeds of outstanding, heroic charity. And she did not die a martyr's death. Many people think she did, but the decree which canonized her makes no mention of her as a martyr. She is St. Joan, Virgin, not St. Joan, Virgin and Martyr. The Church is right; Joan did not die for the Faith. Nor did the voices she heard play any part in her canonization. No private revelations are ever guaranteed by the Church. So what, we may ask, is left? To find out we must ignore much of what has been written about her by her countrymen. By these I do not mean the French scholars whose devoted work has made available the contemporary records concerning her. The men I have in mind belong to that class of Frenchmen whose intellects and emotions are stronger than their common sense. Léon Bloy, for example, nearly always allows his emotions to outrun his intelligence, and never more so than in what he has written about St. Joan. And there are others with minds so ingeniously complex that they are no longer capable of understanding or accepting simplicity. Then we have the perfervid nationalists, those whose every sentence mentions *la gloire* or *la patrie* and who live in a perpetual paroxysm of uncritical patriotism. To them the world outside France is a gray shadowland—if indeed a world outside France can be imagined—and they write of St. Joan with an exalted madness. Even Charles Péguy can make God say: "But with all their faults, I love the French still more than I do all the other peoples who, supposedly, have fewer faults."

The sanctity of St. Joan is a simple thing. Its taproot is obedience to the will of God. If we all obeyed God, we should all be saints. It is as simple as that, which is not to say that it is easy. Such obedience is not the forced, sullen acquiescence we might give to the whims of an earthly tyrant; it is a joyful anticipation of a father's wishes, but it is, too, a matter which needs an iron will and a complete disregard of the promptings of the world.

From the moment Joan heard the voices giving her God's orders she never wavered. She overcame the handicaps of her youth, her sex, her lowly station, her ignorance, and advanced without fear or hesitation toward her goal. She left home and parents, entered the rough, harsh world of war and politics, imposed her will on a vacillating, uncertain king, won hard victories in the field, suffered capture, rigorous imprisonment, trial, and death—all in cheerful, willing obedience to the words of God. Unlike some who believe they are achieving a great design under God's direct orders, she never for one moment neglected to practice the ordinary duties and virtues of the Christian life. She refused to hate the English, the great enemies of her country. Dealing with them collectively, she invariably offered them generous surrender terms, and to individuals she was kind and merciful. Nothing could shake her loyalty—ordinary, human loyalty. She had every excuse for thinking her King had deserted her, yet right to the very end she was always quick to spring to his defense. And loyalty is a great virtue, one very lacking today when Communism uses treachery as a major instrument of policy and, in the West, the betrayal of a friend to gain some great monetary or political advantage is too often regarded as the natural thing to do. She had immense courage, physical and moral, again a virtue of which we are a little short today. And she was high-spirited and cheerful. Like St. Teresa, she believed in cheerfulness, not a superficial, unthinking gaiety, but that happy serenity which is the fruit of perfect trust in God.

A kind, brave, loyal, and cheerful person is someone well worth knowing. When such a person gladly and unflinchingly obeys the will of God, you have a saint. Which is what Joan is. It is not her voices, her battles, or her death which have given her that most high and splendid title; not subtlety of mind, theological learning, or savage austerities, but simply an eagerness to do all things and abandon all things for the love of God.

She was given the great chance of becoming His tool and she co-operated to the utmost of her power. That is why, when the memory of those battles long ago has faded from the history books, people will still turn to her in supplication.

If you have enjoyed this book, consider making your next selection from among the following . . .

Prices subject to change.

Prices subject to change.

Prices subject to change.